G000123175

THE BOSS

HARRY HARRIS

First published in 2019

EMPIRE PUBLICATIONS
1 Newton Street, Manchester M1 1HW
© Harry Harris 2019

ISBN: 978-1-909360-73-0

CONTENTS

ACKNOWLEDGEMENTS

Ash & John at Empire Publications

DEDICATION

To all those long suffering Spurs fans!

FOREWORD

I'VE BEEN ASSOCIATED WITH SPURS AS MAN AND boy and its now 50 years since I first walked through the doors of the club as a schoolboy and excitedly heading off for training there two evenings a week; so I can go all the way back to Bill Nicholson, and have been a player there managed by Terry Neill, who gave me my debut, Keith Burkinshaw, Peter Shreeves and David Pleat.

I've seen those managers create some brilliant teams, and while we won plenty of silverware under Keith Burkinshaw it baffles me to this day how we didn't win more, and at certain times even the league title eluded us.

I was 16 when I was brought into first team training at Cheshunt and first encountered the legendary Billy Nick. I also travelled with the squad to Red Star Belgrade just to gain some experience. Bill Nick watched me play my first game at White Hart Lane. It was for the Tottenham youth team in the FA Youth Cup when I scored a hat trick and we knocked out Middlesbrough in a replay. I told this story about Bill at his Memorial. Bill was held in high esteem, so much respect, and of course, it was well merited, but if you saw him walking toward you in the club's car park, you would dive for cover behind a car, so as not to be noticed, to avoid him at all costs, like the strictest headmaster coming toward you in the school corridors. The next day after my hat trick, there was Bill Nick walking toward me! But, I thought, there was no better time, to actually see the great man himself after such a feat in the youth team, a performance to be proud of and I knew the manager had been watching. Here was a time to puff out your chest and not be afraid to confront the manager. Bill said, 'Ah, young Hoddle, I saw your hat-trick last night". I was eagerly waiting for a 'well done' or a word of encouragement, anything remotely praise worthy. Instead he said, "Your third goal, you should have passed

it, not gone round the keeper, too risky." Well, I was pretty deflated like a balloon, but then again, it showed you the high standards that this manager set and you had to be pretty special to gain any sort of praise. But with my managerial experience, I now know, that he was putting a young upstart in his place, making the point that if you think you did so well, try to do even better.

Later when I got into the first team when Terry Neill was manager, senior players such as Stevie Perryman would tell me that if Bill had said 'well done" to a player, it was like gold dust, something rare, but really special, a bit like a Paul Hollywood handshake in Great British Bake off, but rarer! Terry Neill gave me my debut, but I must confess that it was some shock when a man so steeped in Arsenal's history turned up as Spurs manager. It was indeed a big surprise at the time, and it wasn't too long, just a couple of years, before he moved on to Arsenal to become their manager, but at the time I wasn't dwelling too much on who was the manager, whether the appointment was right or not, I was just a young kid over excited about the prospect of playing for the club I had loved virtually all my life.

Terry had Wilf Dixon as his coach but he also brought Keith Burkinshaw down form Newcastle to be one of his coaches, while Peter Shreeves was my youth team coach. When Keith Burkinshaw took over as manager I was very interested to see how that would work out for him. Back in the day when the assistant or coach you brought in took over as manager it was quite a risk, but Keith very quickly adjusted to his new role. The importance of Peter Shreeves should not be overlooked in Keith's reign. They were totally opposite characters, and while they might not have seemed compatible as individuals, they had the perfect chemistry when it came to working together. Keith had a touch of Bill about him; he was a no nonsense Yorkshireman who didn't hand out praise lightly, it had to be earned, while Peter was the more relaxed, happy go lucky character who would engage with all the players on a one to one basis if necessary to smooth the way for the manager – it was a bit like good cop, bad cop. But Peter was also a very good coach and very capable, and for me it meant I was very comfortable with the new set up having known Peter well as my youth team coach.

Keith surprised everyone, having been relegated, then promoted, he went out and brought Ossie Ardiles and Ricky Villa to Tottenham after the pair had won the World Cup with Argentina. We all were left pondering how that would pan out. As it was, it wasn't as easy as everyone thought to import two world class World Cup winners and off you go. No, there were plenty of ironing out to do, and it took time for them to settle down to a strange country, a different language, and a totally different style of football. It didn't happen overnight, but when it did click after quite a lot of adjustment, we ended up with a wonderful team, and that was down to Keith adding the missing ingredient, a couple of outstanding strikers in Garth Crooks and Steve Archibald, and it shouldn't be underestimated how good Mark Falco was in adding to the fire power up front. They all scored a lot of important goals in a hugely talented and creative team. With so many creative players, we had to find the way to win the ball back and all that took time to put together but once the final pieces of the jigsaw arrived with Crooks and Archibald, it was a great team and wonderful to watch, and in '82 we were in the running for four trophies. We ended up with only the FA Cup but really it should have been much more; we were three minutes away from winning the League Cup and close to winning in Europe but came up against a Barcelona team that kicked lumps out of us; with a stronger referee we would have had at least a couple red carded, and we also threw the league away.

Keith did win two FA Cups and rounded off his reign with the UEFA Cup. He left the next day and that was a travesty. It was wrong. It was all about turning the club into a corporate entity, which didn't fit comfortably with Keith, and the new owners were clearly looking elsewhere for the man who shared their vision for the future. The prospect of Keith building another great team and winning more trophies went out of the window. Peter Shreeves took over for a couple of seasons and he had a reasonably good record, in fact, he could easily have won the league as we played some fantastic football under his management, and came very close again.

David Pleat came in and we really should have won the League for sure in 86/87 in what turned out to be the final season before I left for Monaco. Again the football was fantastic, it was a great season, and even to this day the Spurs fans talk about that team. The manager switched tactics to a 4-5-1 which was ahead of its time, something that you see all the time these days but it was so different it caused teams so many problems they couldn't cope with. Clive Allen played up front and scored 49 goals that season, and we had some magnificently gifted individuals with Chris Waddle, Ossie and myself. It took time to sort out the shape of the team, but it was important that a player of Richard Gough's defensive abilities came into the heart of the defence, and Gary Mabbutt was still there and it was a very strong well balanced side, that played the 'Spurs Style', a joy to watch as well as taking us to the point where we can only look back with regret that we didn't land the title, although we came very close, just didn't quite get over the line. For me it was a pleasure to have played in that team, I played as a No 10 just behind Clive, with two wingers and that was the only season in my entire Spurs playing career that I played as a No 10.

I enjoyed my time with Monaco under a very young Arsene Wenger, returning to manage Swindon and had an opportunity to become Spurs manager, but chose to go to Chelsea instead as there were things happening at Spurs that needed to be cleared up, and I felt it wasn't the right time. But I got a second chance, and when the call came again, this time I couldn't say 'no' even though again I wasn't quite sure about the timing. But here was the club I had supported since the age of eight or nine, I had turned them down once, and didn't know whether the chance would pass me by if I turned them down again. I was at Southampton at the time and we were pretty high up the table about fifth or sixth with an unbelievable run, but it was 'my club' that wanted me and although it was a wrench to leave Southampton in mid-season, I went for it at Spurs not knowing if I would ever get another chance.

It should have been the happiest time of my footballing life, I was manager of Spurs having been a player for so long and enjoyed my time there so much as a player but it turned out to be the unhappiest, and I am not going to dwell on the reason for too long, suffice to say it was a tough and hugely frustrating time for me. I supposed I put extra pressure on myself wanting to do well for the club, and even more pressure from the fans wanting me to succeed and do as well as I did as a player but all I will say is that I didn't have the tools to achieve something, instead there was a lot of politics, and I didn't get all the players I wanted, or indeed needed to have made a success of the job.

Let me now fast forward to the present day and the arrival of Jose Mourinho....

First of all we should all applaud the wonderful work of Mauricio Pochettino, because if it wasn't for the way he turned around Spurs then someone like Mourinho wouldn't have given Spurs a second glance. In fact up until a couple of years ago, it would have been imaginable to think of Mourinho at Spurs. So it's a measure of how well Pochettino has built the team up that the club can attract a manager of Mourinho's calibre and world standing. But it's not only Pochettino, it's the fact that the club also now have a world class training centre and a world class stadium;

all the ingredients to make Spurs an attractive proposition for Mourinho.

The issue with Pochettino was a very simple one, could he get the team over line and win silverware. He came pretty closer with the Champions League, but without any silverware to show for so long in the job, you can see why Daniel Levy thought of bringing in Mourinho, a serial winner.

With all my years in the game, you have a sense when things are coming to the boil, and you could see that there was going to be a change of manager at Arsenal, sooner rather than latter. Daniel Levy could also see that happening and he knew if he hung around too long then Mourinho might be lost to Arsenal, and if not Arsenal, then Bayern Munich or Real Madrid. There was too much speculation, too much going on, and eventually Mourinho would have been snapped up. How long Daniel Levy and the board had been thinking of making a change, who knows, but eventually they had to move quickly with things moving quickly at Arsenal.

So, while there were initially mixed feelings among Spurs fans at losing someone so well liked as Pochettino, the arrival of Mourinho would have given the supporters reason to believe the will deliver silverware at long last. It might only be in the short term as Mourinho has moved on after two or three years, but even so it is what the Spurs fans crave, - trophies. Every Spurs fan, every Spurs player has been waiting to win something, and you can sense that their patience was running out, as indeed it probably run out for Daniel Levy, who must have been sick and tired of everyone banging on about the lack of silverware. The club needs a trophy to move it to the next level.

Yes, it was a shock to see Pochettino go after all that he had done for the club, but if he wants to stay in football, there looks like plenty of openings for him. However, in a way it wasn't a surprise that Daniel Levy was looking to someone like Mourinho.

Hopefully Mourinho will achieve what the Spurs fans desperately want. He has done it everywhere he has gone, so there will be optimism that he will deliver at Spurs. Why not at Tottenham? With the training ground, the stadium and the players at the manager's disposal, it all is there for him to deliver.

If Mourinho does win silverware at Tottenham it will prove to have been the right move at the right time for him to go to Spurs. It will also turn out to be a shrewd move for Mourinho, who will quickly discover that Spurs are a massive club, much bigger than he might have thought. In fact he probably has underestimated just how big a club Spurs are, there is a bigger fan base than at Chelsea, and no one now has better facilities in terms of training ground and stadium.

He has walked into a fantastic job at the right time with Spurs becoming a modern day club with the best stadium and training ground you will find anywhere in world football. This is a good marriage in my view.

Harry Harris actually penned my autobigraphy the year I left Spurs for Monaco, and has written, so he tells me, nearly 90 football books. I am sure his detailed account of Spurs managers through the years will interest every genuine Spurs fan, and might be an eye opener for other clubs' supporters as Jose Mourinho is one of those characters who has universal appeal.

Glenn Hoddle
December 2019

	MANAGER	SPELL(S)	GAMES	WINS	% WIN
1	FRANK BRETTELL	1898–1899	63	37	58.73
2	ARTHUR TURNER	1942–1946	49	27	55.10
3	ANDRÉ VILLAS-BOAS	2012–2013	80	44	55.00
4	MAURICIO POCHETTINO	2014–2019	293	159	54.27
5	JOHN CAMERON	1899–1907	570	296	51.93
6	DAVID PLEAT	1986–1987	119	60	50.42
7	TIM SHERWOOD	2013–2014	28	14	50.00
8	HARRY REDKNAPP	2008–2012	198	98	49.49
9	BILL NICHOLSON	1958–1974	832	408	49.03
10	ARTHUR ROWE	1949–1955	283	135	47.70
11	FRED KIRKHAM	1907–1908	61	29	47.54
12	JIMMY ANDERSON	1955–1958	161	75	46.58
13	PERCY SMITH	1929–1935	253	109	46.38
14	DOUG LIVERMORE & RAY CLEMENCE	1992–1993	51	23	45.09
15	MARTIN JOL	2004–2007	149	67	44.67
16	PETER SHREEVES	1984–1986 & 1991–1992	177	79	44.63
17	JACK TRESADERN	1935–1938	146	65	44.52
18	PETER MCWILLIAM	1913–1927 & 1938–1942	750	331	44.13
19	'THE DIRECTORS'	1908–1913	231	99	42.86
20	JOE HULME	1946–1949	150	64	42.67

INTRODUCTION

TOTTENHAM HOTSPUR'S LAST TROPHY WAS the Carling Cup in 2008 when they defeated Arsenal in the semi-finals and Chelsea in the final. It was their first trophy for nine years, their second in 17. Remember the manager? Juande Ramos. Not a name now regarded as one of the club's greatest ever and, judging by the rankings of the top 20 managers based on percentage results, he doesn't figure anywhere among the 'best".

But looking at that appalling record of failure and zero titles in their recent history for such a so-called bug club, now in a near £1 billion super stadium with state of the art training ground, it beggars belief.

So, it's easy to see why Mauricio Pochettino has been held in such esteem for all his achievements and reaching the Champions League Final for the first time in the club's history, but with the arrival of a serial winner like Jose Mourinho, there is the hope of some silverware at long last. Yet, not everyone approves of Mourinho's appointment, although the chance of some shining silverware might change those hard liners.

The appointment of Mourinho, who infamously swore he'd never mange Spurs out of allegiance and respect for former club Chelsea, and the sacking of one of the most popular managers in the club's history in Pochettino, begged the question who has been Spurs' greatest ever manager and who was the worst?

This book goes in search of those answers prompted by the arrival of the "Mr Marmite of Management", who many still believe is 'The Special One' while just as many are also convinced that he is past his sell-by-date as he returns in his fourth reincarnation in the Premier League after a glittering managerial career that had stalled badly at Manchester United. Mourinho first came to international attention in his native Portugal where he won the European Cup with unfancied Porto. Such was his impact there that he was quickly recruited by Roman Abramovich and guided Chelsea to their first title for 60 years. There followed a season in Milan where he won the treble with an Inter team that had largely been written off in their own country and then he departed for Madrid where his exit seemed to be brought about more by the playing staff and the press than results. His return to Chelsea saw another title and more acrimony before he got the job many thought he was made for – manager of Manchester United, in 2016. Unfortunately, that didn't quite go as planned and he left after two and a half seasons with 'only' a Europa League and League Cup to show for his efforts. No wonder his arrival at the glittering new Tottenham Hotspur Stadium has caused controversy among long suffering Spurs fans. Is he the man to bring the 'glory, glory' years back to Tottenham? Or will he and Levy clash over money?

This book is not a biography of Spurs new boss however. Instead it takes a look at the job as he has just taken. The role of Tottenham boss has seen some great names and some obscure ones. From the great Bill Nicholson and Keith Burkinshaw, through to Terry Venables, Glenn Hoddle, Ossie Ardiles and even the likes of Christian Gross and two Arsenal icons – Terry Neill and George Graham. You couldn't make it up!

It has largely been a revolving door of managers who were hired only for many of them to hear the famous refrain 'You're Fired' from Lord of the Boardroom Alan, now Lord, Sugar who was Spurs chairman between 1991 and 2001. There is a profile of the current Tottenham supremo Daniel Levy who has masterminded the move to a stadium reckoned to be one of the finest in Europe but whose grip on the purse strings many believed hastened Mauricio Pochettino's exit.

Pride of place now goes to Jose Mourinho. I reveal how he was hired, how Pochettino was fired, and all the ramifications of the fall out and the reaction is detailed here. When usually there have been plenty of tomes marvelling at the exploits of a club's "Greatest Ever Players" rarely if at all, are book devoted to Great Managers. But football has evolved to the point that Pep Guardiola, Jurgen Klopp and Jose Mourinho command wages every bit as eye watering as their star players, with headlines to match their touchline exploits.

Erik Thorstvedt, the big former Norway and Spurs keeper, felt bringing in Mourinho for Pochettino didn't make sense to him, and indeed too many others. Thorstvedt, 57, was at the club for Terry Venables' shock move upstairs to take on the role of chief executive, shortly after guiding Spurs to the FA Cup in 1991. "I didn't think it was going to happen. If the sacking was only because of the results, it's incredible really. The down-turn hasn't just been this season, it goes a little bit further back. But I think he would have been able to turn it around. He will be a massive name for Tottenham fans forever. It amazes me how quickly things can turn and this is a prime example. A Champions League final– and now this. We're going to remember his time as the happy days. There has been stability, consistent top-four finishes, the ground, the training ground – the joy that has been there for the fans has been incredible. Now a manager that Tottenham fans have been trained to hate is in charge. And we're going to start hearing Mourinho songs coming from the stands. It's so strange. It will be fascinating to see how it plays out. I don't know if it's going to end well, because it rarely does with Mourinho. But maybe there's a trophy in the cabinet before that all happens." Spurs were already out of the League Cup and out of the Premier League title race when Levy pulled the plug on the Argentinian's five-and-a-half year reign. Thorstvedt added: "The best chance would have to be the FA Cup – that's what Mourinho must target."

Of all the managers mentioned here, it's clear that Billy Nick would be my favourite, my best manager of all-time, someone I cut my journalistic teeth on at the now long defunct *Tottenham Weekly Herald*. But those who have supported Spurs even longer than my near 60 years might consider Arthur Rowe and his wonderful push and run team to be the best and insist that Arthur was even better than Nicholson, who I had the privilege of helping write his autobiography.

Later there was Terry Venables, a genius coach recruited spectacularly by the then owner/chairman Irving Scholar who worked wonders with a team packed with glittering skill, led by Paul Gascoigne who led them to victory over Arsenal in a memorable FA Cup semi-final with that never to be forgotten long range free kick over England 'keeper (and his fishing partner) David Seaman and went on to lift the Cup even with Gazza injured at the start of the Wembley showpiece. As for popular managers, there is a wide choice from Harry Redknapp, Glenn Hoddle, Ossie Ardiles, Keith Burkinshaw/Peter Shreeves, David Pleat, and Martin Jol.

Yet incredibly, Spurs appointed two men steeped in Arsenal tradition: George Graham (1-nil to the Gunners fame) and Terry Neill. How that came about I will let you know later in this book as I was there when it happened and have the inside track. At least George Graham won a trophy but, like Juande Ramos, he could hardly be described as 'popular' with the fans. In fact he might even be rated one of the worst along with the likes of Andre Villa Boas and Tim Sherwood, who got that desperate towards the end of his reign that he invited a fan to manage in his place!

1: POCH OUT, JOSE IN

TOTTENHAM CHAIRMAN DANIEL LEVY announced the sacking of Mauricio Pochettino, the man who had guided Spurs to their first European Cup final in June, at around 19:30 GMT on Tuesday. Shortly after 06:30 GMT the following morning Jose Mourinho was revealed as Pochettino's replacement. Between the sun setting on Tuesday night and rising again on Wednesday morning it was all done, one out, one in. Although, of course, the dynamics of this industry being what they are, behind the scenes much of the ground work had been done days if now weeks earlier.

Jose Mourinho spent the night before the big announcement at a private hotel within the grounds of the Enfield Training Centre after finalising the details of his contract with club officials, and complimented the club on the quality of the pillows. He had clearly slept well. Not so his predecessor, whose exit was far from harmonious, as such departures tend to be.

Daniel Levy's case for appointing the hugely contentious and controversial Jose Mourinho didn't really take much explanation. He said, "In Jose we have one of the most successful managers in football. He has a wealth of experience, can inspire teams and is a great tactician. He has won honours at every club he has coached. We believe he will bring energy and belief to the dressing room."

This was his third Premier League club. The former Chelsea and Manchester United boss signed a contract until the end of the 2022-23 season, the media speculating that he would earn a basic £8m a year rising to a potential £15m with lucrative bonuses including £2m for reaching the top four from the club's lowly position seemingly well out of the running.

"The quality in both the squad and the academy excites me," said the 56-year-old Portuguese in the initial officially manicured statements. "Working with these players is what has attracted me."

Tottenham reached the Champions League final under Pochettino, but lost 2-0 to Liverpool in Madrid. The Argentinian has been appointed in May 2014 and did not win a trophy in his time in charge of the north London club, with Spurs' last silverware being the League Cup in 2008.

Mourinho, who still has a home in London, won three Premier League titles – in 2005, 2006 and 2015 – as well as an FA Cup and three League Cups in two spells at Spurs' rivals Chelsea. Having taken over at Manchester United in May 2016, he won the Europa League and Carabao Cup with them in 2017 but was sacked by the Old Trafford club in December 2018, with the club 19 points behind league leaders Liverpool and had not managed another side before joining Spurs. He has also previously managed Portuguese side Porto, where he won the Champions League in 2004. At Italian club Inter Milan, Mourinho won a league, cup and Champions League treble in 2010 and was named Fifa's world coach of the year, while he led Spanish team Real Madrid to the La Liga title in 2012.

He took over a Spurs side that were without a win in their past five games, slipping to 14th in the Premier League, 20 points behind leaders Liverpool after just 12 matches. Mourinho had turned down a number of managerial opportunities, including in China, Spain and Portugal, since leaving Old Trafford, and being out of work for the previous 11 months. Mourinho apparently told Lyon in October that he already had a job lined up. Were he and Tottenham in discussions back then? Certainly it did according to Lyon President Aulus.

After Mourinho's appointment, Tottenham captain Harry Kane believed he could be the man to end the club's near 12-year wait for a trophy. Mourinho has won 20 major trophies, but Tottenham are without one since the League Cup in 2008. "The gaffer's won at every club he's gone to – there's no hiding away from that," said Kane, who went to see Pochettino at home after his sacking. "I've made it clear that I'm at the stage of my career where I want to win trophies. I've made it clear I want to win them here and it's a big year for us. Realistically we look at the Champions League and the FA Cup this season to try to do that, so we'll see how that goes and then from my point of view I'll keep doing what I'm doing, keep fighting for this club on the pitch.

"We all want to win. We wanted to win when Mauricio was here; we want to win the same now the gaffer's here. But of course when someone's got a reputation like he has, it gives you confidence, it gives you that belief in the team. It's almost a fresh slate for everyone now to show the manager what they can do and hopefully the players can thrive on that." England captain Kane scored 175 goals in 269 games for the club but has no winners' medals.

Under Pochettino, Spurs finished second in the Premier League in 2016-17, runners-up in the 2014-15 League Cup and lost the Champions League final to Liverpool. A poor start to this season, with three wins from their opening 12 games, cost Pochettino. "I wanted to go and see him, and we had a chat for a couple of hours," Kane said of his visit to Pochettino. "It was nice to do that before the new manager came in. It was a big shock on Tuesday night for everyone, the players included, and then it was a quick turnaround. All of a sudden we've got a new manager, one of the best managers there's been in the game, so automatically you have to turn your head towards that and focus on the game."

Pochettino signed Dele Alli from MK Dons in 2015, and the attacking midfielder became key for both Spurs and England. Alli also visited Pochettino following his sacking and spoke to him as a friend. "It's clear to everyone how much Poch meant to the players. As soon as I found out the news I was very upset and I went to see him the next day. It was a conversation between two friends."

Eric Dier believed Mourinho was the "perfect" replacement for Pochettino, "His record is unbelievable and he transmits that confidence. The way he speaks, you believe it, you feel it from him. I hope we can win a lot of games and do as well as possible. I think he's the perfect person to have followed on from Pochettino. We're really happy that if someone was to replace Pochettino it was him, with that winning mentality. Before we were trying to win trophies and nothing will change. I think, for everyone, we're very lucky to have played under Pochettino and now Mourinho. We couldn't be luckier."

Tottenham play-maker Son Heung-min wrote a heartfelt message on Instagram about the departure of Mauricio Pochettino: "Needless to say how much I thank this man. Words are powerless to express my gratitude. I have learned a lot from you not only in football, but in life. Good luck in your future and I wish you all the best."

Tottenham's Belgium defender Toby Alderweireld said: "We came a long way together. A lot of players achieved big things. I can see where we've come from before my time at Spurs. We have to be thankful for what he achieved at the club. We have to try to work hard and I think there will be a (new) manager quickly. Spurs are a big club so there will be a big manager for us. We (the players) have to stay together and change things as quickly as possible."

The Tottenham Hotspur Supporters' Trust were "shocked and saddened" at the decision to remove Pochettino from his post and were critical of the club's board. They said in a statement: "During his time at Spurs, Poch gave us many of our best moments as supporters, made Tottenham Hotspur a force to be reckoned with again, and forged a strong link with the fans. We will never forget the joy he brought us. But many fans thought Poch had earned the right to turn it around in the first sustained period of poor form we've had during his time at the club. We now have to look forward and take stock. But there are questions that must be asked of the board of THFC. The club's statement makes it clear the board has decided to sack the manager and coaching staff. It is their decision. We question why this decision was taken at the end, rather than the beginning, of the international break. We question whether the timing of the decision leaves the club with much choice in who takes over."

Former Spurs and England striker Gary Lineker felt the club would not find a "better replacement", adding on Twitter: "He (Pochettino) helped the club to punch massively above their weight for years." Paul Gascoigne added, "Jose Mourinho is a unbelievable manager, if I was a Tottenham player I would be delighted knowing he was coming in. For me Sir Alex Ferguson and Sir Bobby Robson were the very best and Jose Mourinho is not far from them, you cannot get much better than him. I don't think it will take him long to win round the dressing room. If I was a player I would look at what he has won, the emotions that he incites in players, he is a manager I would play for certainly. He will put the players on their toes certainly. Jose will want to strengthen his team to get it to the standard of Liverpool and Manchester City. He won't want to mess about."

Former Tottenham captain Gary Mabbutt said of the appointment, "I think everyone at the club will always have great affection for Mauricio but as a board of directors you have to look at that way things are going and the board had to make a decision. I was one of the managers of one of the teams competing in an exhibition match when they were testing out the new stadium in March. Jose was part of the coaching staff looking after an Inter Milan XI. He was great throughout the day and afterwards he came to me and said how much this club is moving forward, how fantastic this stadium is. He was clearly very impressed."

Former Tottenham striker Eidur Gudjohnsen, who played under Mourinho at Chelsea added, "I have great respect for the man. He took us to another level at Chelsea. It is a big challenge to move into that top level but Tottenham should always be challenging the top four."

Former Spurs legend Micky Hazard took to Twitter to say, "I would just like to thank Mauricio and his team for the wonderful memories they gave us all and it's been a real pleasure knowing you and being part of the last 5 years. Best wishes to you all wherever you go and you will always be remembered and welcome here in Tottenham. COYS"

Former Spurs centre-forward Peter Crouch said: "If anyone deserved time, it was him. I thought it [his dismissal] was shocking." However Crouch had to accept Levy's reasons for sacking Pochettino as he added, "The results speak for themselves. The Champions League final papered over a few cracks at the end of last season, as much as I like Pochettino. People are saying these players all have a relationship with Pochettino. But if I was a player, I'd love to work with Mourinho. I'd absolutely love it."

Former Tottenham winger and now BBC 5Live commentator Chris Waddle said of the sacking, "This has shocked the football world but it is a results business. I still think the mistake was not to get rid of Christian Eriksen, Toby Alderweireld and Jan Vertonghen, who are out of contract. When you get players who are running out of contract, mentally and physically they have found it hard. They are a fit group. Mauricio Pochettino has done a marvellous job, he has not freshened it as he wanted to, the stadium cost an absolute fortune and he has kept hold of players he wanted to move on. Unfortunately Tottenham cannot stand still, they cannot be a team in 10th to 14th place in the Premier League. They were in the Champions League final last season, in the top four the last four years running and he has been a big part of it. They have looked at it and thought, where are Tottenham going at the moment? Finishing 10th is not going to pay the bills or attract the big players"

On the new boss Waddle added, "Is he a Tottenham-type manager? Will he sort it out? Will he be a fans' favourite with his style? I would say not, unless he changes his philosophy. Carlo Ancelotti would have been a better fit - he has won as a player and a manager. Football moves very quickly, eventually it happens. He [Pochettino] has been brilliant for the club but the way they have developed, they cannot stand still."

Match of the Day's Alan Shearer said of the quick turnaround, "They say nothing should surprise you in football but it has moved really quickly. I was surprised by Pochettino's sacking, you would think what he has achieved in the five years - turning them into regular top-four contenders and visitors to the knock-out stages of the Champions League - that he would have something in the bank, that he would be given a few months to turn things around. Mourinho has been waiting for a big job and now has got one. He has big boots to fill to try and better what Pochettino has done. The Argentine may not have won a trophy but by the way that Pochettino delivered his football and that Champions League final was very special and will live with Spurs fans for many years.

Former England boss Sam Allardyce felt certain that Mourinho would thrive at Spurs, "There were often questions that because he lived in the hotel at Manchester United that was one of the problems, because he was away from his family. He's back with his family, back in London, which he loves, and he's back with Tottenham, which is a massive club for him to get his teeth into and try to get them winning some trophies. Certainly he's got the talent and quality of squad to make Tottenham a big challenger and I think they can still challenge for the top four."

Mourinho's appointment during the cut and thrust of a General Election campaign so it was only right that the local MP, David Lammy, had his say, "Tottenham is only about 4 square miles large, we will struggle to contain Mourinho's ego which is bigger than even our new stadium!"

Further afield Jurgen Klopp told the press he felt Mourinho was 'desperate' to get back to Premier League management while praising the work of Pochettino. "Welcome back, Jose," Klopp said. "Obviously it's nice to have him back. He was desperate, you could see the time he was not in. But on the other side Mauricio is not there any more and that shows you how things change so quickly nowadays. About five months ago we played each other in the Champions League final and now he is on holiday – I hope he can enjoy it. He did a brilliant job at Tottenham, no one doubts that, an outstanding coach but everyone knows that pretty much all the jobs available – and not available – Mauricio will be in contention. When I heard it first I could not believe in that moment, but a couple of moments later there was already a solution. Jose? He is highly motivated, so it will be interesting as well."

Pep Guardiola, who duelled with the former Real Madrid boss when managing Barcelona and Manchester City, described his rival as an "incredible manager". "I think you know him better than me," he said. "He was many years here with different clubs. Welcome back. He is an incredible manager and I'm pretty sure he'll do a good job."

Newcastle boss Steve Bruce commented: "I'm delighted that Jose's back because when he walked into the Premier League all them years ago he was a breath of fresh air wasn't he - he was something different. When you look at his records, what he's done, the achievements he's got... I seen it yesterday the trophies he's won, everywhere he's been he's won a league. He's quite remarkable in what he's done, he's up there with as good as you're ever gonna get. The disappointment of course is that Pochettino's gone and if can get the sack then all of us are goosed as far as I'm concerned."

Bournemouth manager Eddie Howe, who had been one of the media's favourites for the job had no doubt Mourinho still had what it takes. "I was as surprised as everybody else watching from afar what happened this week, but Jose is an unbelievable manager and I think it's great for the league that he's back. It's probably not ideal timing for us to go to Tottenham in his first (home) league game. Look at his record. I'd love his track record, the trophies that he's won, the things he's achieved in the game, it's incredible. So, for me, he's one of the all-time greats. I think the trophy cabinet says that. He's certainly got a lot more to give."

It was rumoured Brendan Rodgers had been Levy's first choice, and that the Leicester City boss newly arrived from Celtic had been sounded out after taking his new club to within striking distance of the summit of the Premier League. It was even reported in some sections of the media that Spurs had initially tried to sound out whether the former Liverpool boss would be open to moving to North London, but any attempt to persuade the Foxes to allow Rodgers to leave would be impossible. RB Leipzig's Julian Nagelsmann was also considered. Asked about the rumours, Rodgers replied, "There's nothing to talk on it. This game is full of gossip and speculation. The only thing I would say is I was very happy here at Leicester. I've literally just joined the club in February and everything has been great since we've been in. We have a project here which we want to develop over the next number of years. My sole focus – along with my team, staff and the club here – has been that. In this game, what I've learned, is that you will always be linked with jobs and speculation around other jobs but what's most important is the now and I'm very, very happy here to develop and work with the club in order to help the club develop and improve.'

The FA top brass were delighted at Mourinho's appointment as there had been concern that the club would approach Gareth Southgate had they left the job open to him for after the European Championships in the summer. Southgate has a contract with the FA until 2022, but raised the prospect of an earlier departure if he was no longer feeling 'warmth' from his employers and the fans after the tournament.

Of Pochettino's departure Martin Keown suggested that perhaps the writing had been on the wall for some time, "Pochettino did not sound to me like a company man. He was talking about leaving after the Champions League, and there were comments this week about going back to Spain. Those sorts of things… Arsene Wenger would never have talked unnecessarily like that." Meanwhile Stan Collymore brought up Jose's habit for taking teams a long way over a short period of time but then leaving a mess behind,

"Amazing how some have bought into "Mourinho the winner" without any regard for how he leaves clubs. Unbalanced, fractured, overspending, soulless. Everything Spurs tried to avoid. Good luck, I like Spurs a lot, but it's not how this man comes in, it's how he'll leave you."

Guillem Balague, Spanish football journalist on BBC Radio 5 live said of the appointment, "The timing is a little strange I think. None of Pochettino's backroom staff saw this coming even in the early afternoon of yesterday. It feels like Daniel Levy and Mauricio Pochettino reached the end of the road. Mauricio has been warning for two years that the team needed recycling and he wanted the club to make smarter, faster decisions in the transfer market. It was not just about the amount of money being spent but how they were approaching the transfer market. I think, with the new stadium, Tottenham needed a name to promote the value of the club and Mourinho is certainly that. But I guarantee you if that Levy puts the same restrictions on Mourinho that Pochettino has there will be trouble. And quickly."

BBC sports editor Dan Roan commented: "Spurs have never hired a manager as expensive or demanding as Mourinho, nor spent the kind of money on players that he became accustomed to at clubs such as Real Madrid and Manchester United. But Spurs have come a long way in recent years under Pochettino. They have a new £1bn stadium and training ground, and spent four successive seasons in the Champions League. They now have a European pedigree, and a hugely talented squad. Mourinho has been out of the game for almost a year but retained a home in London. His tribulations at Manchester United saw him lose his 'Special One' status, but his many achievements in the game still command widespread respect. Mourinho will earn £15m a year in wages, double what Pochettino was being paid."

The Times' Matt Lawton said of the managerial swap, "I don't think Mourinho is such a ridiculous appointment. He needs strong leadership above him, for sure, and at Spurs that at least exists in a way it didn't at United. He's also a serial winner. There are obvious concerns but I'd argue he's worth the gamble."

Paul Hayward, "Mourinho will love Tottenham's pre-match videos about the swashbuckling heroes of White Hart Lane. 'To Dare is to Do.' Or, 'Don't You Dare,' as Mourinho prefers to say."

During his time at Spurs, Mauricio Pochettino had a net spend of £109m over five-and-a-half years at Tottenham. Jose Mourinho almost matched that over a 12-week period in 2018 at Manchester United. To many it represented an extraordinary gamble from Daniel Levy.

Michael Cox, "Yes Mourinho wins trophies, but look at his last four jobs (Inter, Real, Chelsea, Man Utd) and the level of success has decreased each time, while the shambles he's left behind has increased each time. That's not a promising pattern."

ESPN's Melissa Reddy believed that Mauricio Pochettino's success in changing perceptions about Tottenham being perennial underachievers is worth any number of trophies. "Mauricio Pochettino made exceeding expectations the norm at Tottenham under several restrictions at a time when their rivals have never been so well resourced or relentless. He changed how we viewed Spurs. A transformation greater than trophies by a certified elite manager."

Adam Crafton, "Tottenham are a club with a modest budget, a chairman who has strong opinions, a long term plan and a lot of players agitating over their future. Every one is a red flag when set against the name Jose Mourinho."

New York Times reporter Tariq Panja believed that Jose Mourinho needs his Spurs stint to be a success for his long-term reputation, "Two jobs ago when a club's fan base was genuinely excited that Mourinho was coming to be their new manager. Rehabilitation job for his reputation as much as it is to fix broken Spurs - kind of remarkable given how much he's won."

Arsenal fan Piers Morgan commented: "My first reaction was, 'I hope they don't get Mourinho', because I would like Mourinho at Arsenal. My second was, 'Well if they get Mourinho, can we have Pochettino?' Arsenal fans want anyone but Emery. You've got Mourinho there, waiting to be hired. We didn't hire him. If Arsenal genuinely want to be competitive and ruthless, they'd pull a Sol

Campbell (who left Spurs for them in 2001) and get Pochettino."

Speaking to BBC Radio 5 Live, The Last word on Spurs podcast's Ricky Sacks, said: "Maybe we have sold our soul to the devil to some degree, but it is a big statement. The board have been accused in the past of not wanting to go to the next level in terms of winning trophies and now they have brought in a man with a proven track record of bringing trophies wherever he has gone. He is used to managing top clubs. The last few hours have happened so quickly, in terms of Mauricio Pochettino leaving and Mourinho coming in, but we have to get behind him.

"Anyone employing Jose as their manager would be having that chat about what is available and what the club are looking for. Jose spoke beforehand about his next club having a clear structure and the board will make it clear as to the funds available to him. His statement says he is looking forward to working with this group and there is a lot of talent there, we have still got over half the season and we can finish in that top with the FA Cup and Champions League to play.

"He will split opinion among the fans but he is a serial winner and we will command the respect of the dressing room straight away. We are missing glory and he is the man that delivers that. It is the biggest gamble in Levy's reign at the club."

2: JOSE MOURINHO

WHEN TOTTENHAM HOTSPUR REACHED the 2019 Champions League Final under Mauricio Pochettino, many Spurs fans felt he was untouchable. Having been used to football chaos and catastrophe down the years, Pock had taken them to the Promised Land of the final of the biggest club tournament in the world and the vast majority assumed that he would be at Spurs for the rest of his days.

Yet despite all the plaudits and success in helping Tottenham finally regain their rightful place at the top table of English football (and even go beyond that by becoming one of the best clubs in Europe) and despite all the great notices about his style of football, defeat in the final in Madrid in June meant that Poch still hadn't landed Spurs any silverware since being appointed in May 2014. So when the team hit a slump in the autumn of 2019 it didn't take long for the board to act.

Chairman Daniel Levy knew The Special One was available. Jose Mourinho wins trophies, it's a simple as that and Tottenham, from boardroom to supporters, are desperate for silverware. Levy said that Mourinho "has a wealth of experience, can inspire teams and is a great tactician. He has won honours at every club he has coached. We believe he will bring energy and belief to the dressing room."

Mourinho still had a home in London and won three Premier League titles – in 2005, 2006 and 2015 at Chelsea. Having taken over at Manchester United in May 2016, he won the Europa League and Carabao Cup with them in 2017. Mourinho was sacked by the Old Trafford club in December 2018, with the club 19 points behind league leaders Liverpool, and had not managed another side before joining Spurs.

He came to prominence winning the Champions League with Portuguese side Porto in 2004, and was first approached by Roman

Abramovich while the incumbent at the Bridge, the hugely popular Italian coach Claudio Ranieri was preparing for his own Champions League semi-final with Monaco. At Italian club Inter Milan, Mourinho won a league, cup and Champions League treble in 2010 and was named Fifa's world coach of the year, while he led Spanish team Real Madrid to the La Liga title in 2012.

Mourinho had turned down a number of managerial opportunities, including in China, Spain and Portugal, since leaving Old Trafford, and had been 11 months without a job.

Of all the managers to have taken charge in the Premier League, Jose Mourinho is still the quickest to reach both the 50-win (63 games) and 100-win (142 games) landmarks in the competition.

Mourinho was only 10 wins away from reaching 200 Premier League victories as a manager when he took charge at Tottenham. Only four managers have won 200 or more games in the Premier League: Sir Alex Ferguson (528), Arsene Wenger (476), Harry Redknapp (236) and David Moyes (204).

And, despite a disastrous final season at Manchester United, Mourinho still had the fifth-best points-per-game ratio of any Premier League manager to have overseen fifty games or more.

Pep Guardiola - 2.39 points per game
Sir Alex Ferguson - 2.16 points per game
Antonio Conte - 2.14 points per game
Jurgen Klopp - 2.12 points per game
Jose Mourinho - 2-10 points per game

He took over a Spurs side that were without a win in their past five games and an away league win since January who had slipped to 14th in the Premier League. They were 20 points behind leaders Liverpool after just 12 matches. With eight domestic league titles, eight domestic cups and four major European trophies, it was easy to see why Tottenham appointed Jose. For Levy and their board the next step was to turn all of Pochettino's enormous potential into silverware, something that has been missing for nearly 12 years,

Mourinho has had a chequered career. It may be full of trophies but it also measure packed with controversy and littered with acrimonious departures. He has collected significant sums in severance pay at every club he's managed. The longest he's stayed at any of his clubs was three years, although he had a total of five at Chelsea across two spells. His troubled reign at United included accusations of dull, pragmatic football and clashes with key players, but after 11 months out of work, which had given him time to reflect and to concentrate on his strengths and try to repair some of the damage he can inflict at the same time, it was felt he would come back stronger than ever.

Many outsiders might assume that for a club without a league title since 1961, and whose last trophy was the 2008 League Cup, that a move for Mourinho would be cause for celebration, with the very strong likelihood of a piece of silverware finally arriving at the club, given that Mourinho has won something at every club bar União de Leiria, the tiny club where he began his managerial career.

However many Spurs have questioned the move or Mourinho, claiming that the club are looking for short term glory rather than building a team fit to grace their brand new stadium in the long term.

During his four and a half years, Pochettino transformed the 'Spursy' stigma that had afflicted the club and recruited or brought through a super fit looking squad. Poch's high pressing game transformed the football as he turned Spurs into an entertaining Top 4 outfit capable of winning anywhere. Yet silverware eluded him as Spurs lost the 2015 League Cup final to Chelsea and were beaten by Liverpool in the Champions League showpiece, and finished second in the Premier League in 2017 behind Leicester City. Suddenly this season that soft underbelly reappeared and it was perhaps the frightening prospect of returning to that 'Spursy' state of lacking a real fighting spirit that hastened the end for the popular Argentine. Some felt the squad had been listening to the same voice for far too long and it was time for a change.

By this point Mourinho, a regular on Sky Sports football coverage, was getting itchy feet and was eager to start work at his eighth club. For a born winner like Jose, pontificating about the shortcomings of others was never going to entertain him for long. Quite simply, he's too good to be a pundit.

Mourinho's honours read like a who's who of the biggest trophies in club football. Besides two Champions Leagues, two UEFA Cups, three Premier League titles, a La Liga title and a Serie A title, he has also won the main domestic cup competition in all four of the countries in which he has managed and three League Cups in England.

He is also the only manager to have won both the Champions League and the UEFA Cup more than once – winning both with Porto, the former with Inter and the latter with Manchester United. As it stands, he has more honours than his new club by 20 to 17!

In 14 completed seasons as a manager, Mourinho has only finished outside the top three of the league in which he is managing once. The only time he has left a club in a position lower than sixth was when Chelsea sacked him in 2016 with the side 16th. His win percentage across his entire career is an impressive 64.8%, picking up a coveted 2.15 points per game on average.

In the Premier League, he has won 61.9% of his matches. Only four managers to have taken charge of 50 or more games in the competition can better his 2.10 points per game – Manchester City boss Pep Guardiola (2.39), former United manager Sir Alex Ferguson (2.16), ex-Chelsea boss Antonio Conte (2.14) and Jurgen Klopp of Liverpool (2.12). Pochettino's points-per-game average was 1.79.

When Mourinho breezed into English football he seemed to be a breath of fresh air. His first news conference at Chelsea in 2004 set the tone as he proclaimed himself 'The Special One'. In the four books I've written about him since I described him as a modern day Brian Clough; abrasive, arrogant, but a genius as a motivator of star players, a brilliant tactician, and a serial winner. All these ingredients made him popular in west London during a first spell in which his Chelsea team dominated the league for two seasons, setting a new record points total in the process. Rivals grudgingly admired his ability to back up the press conference talk on the pitch and, but for the 'ghost goal' at Anfield he would have led them to a Champions League final. Yet by the end of his first spell at Stamford Bridge, unsavoury incidents were intertwined with his winning mentality that soured his relationship with the neutral fan; now you either love him or hate him. It is a pattern that has continued wherever he has managed. The big question now for Spurs fans is whether he can retain all the good ingredients and dispense with the bad. Has he learned the art of sticking around at a club for longer than three seasons? Or do we have to accept that some of his antics are just his style?

Fifteen years on from that startling entrance, his growing army of critics, many of them in the media, claim he is no longer the same force. For a start, his own brand of football is no longer in vogue. Chelsea were built on incredibly solid foundations, his 2005 title winners conceding just 15 goals in 38 games. Their defence was so good that opponents knew that going a goal down was tantamount to losing the game. Yet 15 seasons on and the Premier League has been transformed into a riot of ultra attacking football as clubs attempt to ape the tactics of Messrs Klopp and Guardiola at the top of the league. No longer do teams feel safe parking the bus and, as Mourinho found out during his spell at Old Trafford, the fans don't want to pay to watch 1-0 wins and goalless draws. With high ticket prices and a different clientele comes the need to entertain.

Yet, despite all the negativity that surrounded him at United, he still won two trophies in two full seasons and then claimed that finishing second in the Premier League in 2018-19 points, behind a record-breaking Manchester City team, was his greatest managerial achievement! Well that was Mourinho at his most obtuse, as he claimed it was an incredible feat of management because of all the factors working against him and the squad he had to work with, although supporters would claim he brought a lot of it on himself with some highly questionable signings and terrible man-management.

His critics will point to the bible of the modern game, statistics. They seem to indicate that his powers are on the wane, as his win percentage (53.8%) and points-per-game ratio (1.89) at United were the lowest of his managerial career since his first job at Leiria in the Portuguese Liga between July 2001 and January 2002.

Yet, remarkably that points-per-game number was exactly the same as that achieved by Pochettino during the same period at Tottenham, and while United's vast majority of fans were glad to see the back of Mourinho there was an outpouring of weeping and wailing when Pochettino was shown the door! It just goes to show the difference the style of football can make.

There are more stats which indicate his decline: Since leaving Real Madrid in the summer of 2013, Mourinho has won 58.6% of competitive games and 56.8% of league matches. From the start of his managerial career at Benfica to the end of his spell at Madrid, he had won 67.6% of competitive fixtures and 70.8% of league games. However, the stats can equally be used to show that Mourinho can still be management's main man, he is the go to boss if you want to win major trophies, a rare talent in this day and age.

Mourinho remains the fastest manager to reach both 50 and 100 wins in Premier League history. However his 50th win with United came in his 92nd game. His total of 176 Premier League points with United was fewer than four other teams during his time at Old Trafford, including Tottenham! Mourinho's United side scored fewer goals than all of their main rivals during this time – 151, a disturbing 83 goals fewer than that scored by Manchester City during the same period, a statistic which goes some way to explaining his dismissal in December 2018.

In turning to "one of the most successful managers in football" who "has won honours at every club he has coached", Levy also appointed perhaps the most talked about manager in world football. Some wags have even claimed that Spurs' manager is now bigger than the club he has joined, as evidenced by his first press conference which was over-flowing with media of all sorts from all corners of the globe. And, while Jose's record at United must be a concern, it is still the exception rather than the rule; perhaps the club was too big and the tradition too strong, even for Jose. Now at Tottenham, where fans will perhaps be more accepting if he brings them some glory, he will get a little more leeway.

Mourinho has a compelling track record of starting strongly with clubs, and always seems to deliver in his first season, but it is rare for him to move into a club in mid season without the benefit of preparing his players for the season ahead and perhaps recruiting new ones.

Mourinho won 11 of his first 16 league games to win the Portuguese title in his debut season with Porto and lost just once en route to guiding Chelsea to the Premier League title in his first season in England. He suffered only four defeats in his first successful Serie A campaign with Inter and failed to win only nine of 38 matches in his first La Liga season at Real Madrid.

Mourinho's first opponent as Spurs boss was West Ham United whom he had beaten 11 times before - the third most victories he has achieved against a club. The team he'd beaten the most in his career, a total of 13 times; why, that would be Tottenham, of course!

Mourinho praised the quality of his squad, their "world class" stadium and training ground in his first comments, albeit, sanitised through the club on line sources. "I couldn't be happier and look forward to the challenge," he said.

In his interview with Spurs TV he said: "What can I promise? Passion, real passion. Passion for my job, but also passion for my club, that's the way I have been all my career and I want to try, obviously, everything to bring happiness to everyone who loves the club.

"Even as an opponent, there was always huge respect between me and the club," added Mourinho. "I met you in cup finals, in semi-finals, in big matches and to keep that respect was probably in the back of my mind that one day I could be one of you."

Speaking about the squad he inherited, Mourinho praised the club for keeping their best players and he was looking forward to working with the academy players. "It's a privilege when a manager goes to a club and feels that happiness in relation to the squad he is going to have. It didn't happen many times. To be honest, the majority of the times we go to clubs and we always think 'I like some, I don't like enough' and you think immediately about what to do to change, what to do to make an approach between your ideas and the profile of the players. This is a completely different case. I really like this squad."

There was praise for Spurs £1bn stadium that opened in March, and the club's magnificent training facilities, a testimony to the achievements of their chairman. "I think you are too humble when you say, 'beautiful stadium', too humble. You have to say the best stadium in the world. That's the reality. The training ground is second to none. It probably can only be compared with some American Football training grounds. You cannot compare it with European football at any level, and I've been in the majority of the best places."

THE NEW BACKROOM STAFF

Joao Sacramento - Assistant manager - Portuguese

Lille were far from happy about losing their 44-year-old assistant manager. Sacramento came straight in as Mourinho's right-hand man. He is highly rated within European football. After studying for a degree in Glamorgan, he joined the Welsh FA as a performance analyst - working under Gary Speed and Chris Coleman. In 2014 he joined Monaco as a technical assistant, working there for two years, before being appointed by Lille in January 2017 when current owner Gerard Lopez bought the club but he was sidelined under Marcelo Bielsa during the Argentinian's disastrous spell as head coach of Lille. When Bielsa was sacked, Sacramento took temporary charge along with another coach Fernando da Cruz and then worked as new manager Christophe Galtier's assistant, playing a big part in the club's revival, from escaping relegation to qualifying for the Champions League. Lille Captain Adama Soumaoro told *L'Equipe* that Sacramento's coaching sessions were more enjoyable than Bielsa's and forward Ezequiel Ponce (now at Spartak Moscow) praised him for keeping things simple. He was instrumental as the club finished in the top two for the first time in 14 years last season and was viewed as a future first team manager later on in his career. He came highly recommended by Lille's "sporting advisor" Luis Campos, a close friend of Mourinho's, who was often seen at Lille games during the previous 11 months. He speaks English, French and Spanish.

Carlos Lalin - Chief fitness coach - Venezuelan

Carlos started his career at Deportivo La Coruna, before joining Real Madrid and meeting Mourinho. The 49-year-old fitness coach impressed Mourinho with his methodology and went with Mourinho on his return to Chelsea and then Manchester United. He is credited by Mourinho for getting Diego Costa back in shape at Stamford Bridge, however a bust-up with Mourinho at United in March 2017 saw Lalin storm out of training. However they have clearly since made up! Lalin's time at United came to an end when Mourinho was sacked.

Nuno Santos - Goalkeeper coach - Portuguese

Another casualty for Lille, the 46-year-old was at 14 clubs during his career as a player, including Leeds in the 1998-99 season. After retiring he became goalkeeping coach for Canada, as well as working in their youth set-up. He will now work closely with Hugo Lloris, as the Frenchman bids to make his return for Tottenham after a nasty elbow injury.

Ricardo Formosinho - Scout and analyst - Portuguese

The 63-year-old earned one cap for Portugal as a player, before going into management and taking charge of 21 teams, including a spell in charge of Kuala Lumpur. He was assistant coach and scout at United under Mourinho and departed along with the boss in December 2018 and had been without a club since.

Giovanni Cerra - Chief Analyst - Italian

A former employee at Microsoft, the 43-year-old worked under Mourinho at United as an analyst, scouting data on opponents and helping to develop game-plans. Mourinho publicly berated him in the Old Trafford dug-out during a Europa League game in 2016 after Zorya Luhansk changed their line-up and United's players were left confused. He departed United along with Mourinho.

Lille manager Christophe Galtier criticised Mourinho for taking his coaching staff just days before his side faced Paris Saint-Germain in Ligue 1. "Each has their way of doing things. He called Luis. I don't know if it's [a knife in the back], but it's very classy to do things like that… I was annoyed, frustrated because the timing isn't good. Each will judge the way things are done. What's most important is that I agree with the decision the president took. To be totally transparent, my president informed me of the situation and told me he would let Joao and Nuno go. After a long talk, I understand his decision. It's a shame, the timing is very bad. That's how football is these days but what can he do against two people who want to leave and exit the project for something else? He gave them that possibility. He couldn't do anything else."

Mourinho did not use his long-term agent Jorge Mendes to broker the deal with Spurs. The Portuguese super-agent, who has guided his career since he was a little-known coach at Porto had brokered all of Mourinho's moves since he left Porto in 2004, taking him to Chelsea, Inter Milan, Real Madrid, back to Chelsea and finally to Manchester United. Instead, a three-and-a-half-year contract worth £52million was brokered by Pini Zahavi, who has worked closely with Mendes in the past. Mourinho was represented by Daniel Lorenz, another Portuguese agent, who runs Lorenz Consulting. Mourinho was annoyed when Mendes released a statement on December 7 saying United were happy with the manager, which was the source of much embarrassment, because he was sacked 11 days later! Mourinho publicly backtracked on the Mendes statement on December 11, although he still used him to negotiate his severance package from United later that month. "I've nothing to do with the statement," Mourinho said at the time, "It is Jorge's statement; it is not my statement. I didn't know at all and I don't care about it."

Jose had may have taken a break from football management but that didn't mean he took a complete break from football. In an exclusive interview with the *Radio Times,* Sky Sports football presenter David Jones talked about working with Mourinho in the weeks leading up to his top flight return. Asked whether Mourinho was itching for a return to management, Jones revealed, "Oh, from day one – absolutely. I had lunch with Jose just before the start of the season because he wanted to know what we were about and I wanted to know where he was coming from and it was very clear that this is a guy who considers himself an elite manager who was purely on an enforced sabbatical. If truth be known, we probably had him for longer than we expected to because he was being linked with jobs from day one. What we were able to do on Sky was show the kind of personality and charisma he has that has drawn football clubs to him in the first place.

"What really impressed me was the detailed level of analysis, but beyond that, his ability to explain it in a simplified way that we could get, the viewers could get, and that footballers could get as well."

Jones was one of the few to consistently work alongside Mourinho between management jobs, and was quick to praise the new Spurs boss for getting stuck in with the Sky team. "We're very professional when the red light is on when we have to deliver our analysis," Jones said, "Off-camera you see quite different aspects to personalities. When Mourinho joined us he was very much part of the gang, a barrel of fun. He's very different to his on-screen persona. There was a slightly surreal moment when we were watching Liverpool v Man City. We'd done quite a heavyweight build-up, then we've got Roy Keane tearing up little bits of paper in the corner of the studio organising the sweepstake for us, and Jose's trying to work out which scorelines have already gone so he can work out which scorelines he wants to pick. That kind of fun you have in any office or pub environment is the same we have in the studio. He always stressed that he wanted to be part of the team.

"I assured him I would treat him in the same way as everybody else. He sat with us, ate with us on the catering bus, he joined in that sweep with Roy Keane and everybody, he loved that camaraderie off-camera. But like everyone else at times I had to put him on the spot and in those moments that's when we saw him at his best."

Jones believes Mourinho will provide a terrific boost for Spurs in the short term, but feared he may hit a roadblock with chairman Daniel Levy, "For me it's a huge shock that he would choose Spurs and that Daniel Levy would choose him, knowing what strong forthright characters they both are. I think there will be a short-term jump, but I would think long term Jose's going to find himself having the same problems with the squad and people out of contract as Pochettino did. It will be very interesting to see what happens when we get through to January, what kind of impact he's going to have in terms of the rebuild."

One of the showpiece matches for Sky is Mourinho's Tottenham hosting former protégé Frank Lampard and his young Chelsea team. Jones believes Mourinho would relish the chance to get one over Lampard. "If Lampard's able to go and win at Spurs, that would certainly show Jose! A test of The Humble One. Having said that, Jose would love nothing more than to go up against one of his protégées and put him in his place. That's going to be fascinating."

THE SPECIAL ONESIE

It was standing room only as The Special one, or rather the Special Onesie, breezed into his first media conference dressed in lavender, looking trim, tanned and smiling…yes, actually smiling and even teasing some of the journalists present.

He even failed to walk out in one of his fits of anger when questioned about his previous derogatory comments about never wanting to ever be Spurs manager. Instead he was even happy to talk about his love affair with his new club's jim-jams, and the expensive velvet cushions that gave him such a good night's sleep at the training ground before his unveiling to the world's media.

Mourinho once said he'd never take the Spurs job because "I love Chelsea supporters too much" before the 2015 Capital One Cup final between his Chelsea side and Mauricio Pochettino's Spurs, Mourinho admitted that an exit clause forbade him from managing in England for two years and that even Spurs' attempts to pay compensation to the Blues fell short. "I couldn't go," after confirming the approach from Spurs. "I couldn't train in England for two years." Asked then if he would have considered Spurs, Mourinho added: "No, because I love Chelsea supporters too much."

Mourinho arrived at Tottenham with three Premier League titles at Chelsea and is still heavily associated with the west London club, although the majority of their fans drew the line when he signed for their London rivals Spurs. Inevitably, those acidic comments came back to haunt him, as the media were quick to pick up on them in the immediate aftermath of his appointment. It was something he didn't shy away from when, inevitably, it cropped up in the first media briefing of his reign

"That was before I was sacked!" he explained. "This is modern football. When my father played, the same players played for the same club for 15-20 years. In society now everything is fast, even relationships are fast, players get tired of each other, of the manager. I went to Manchester United with a free mind and a free heart, I loved the fans, the people who worked in the club, and now it is about Spurs and there is no bigger fan than me in the world. Nobody wants Tottenham to win more than me. We cannot win the Premier League this season, but we can win it next season. Not will, but can. I understand people will look at me, like when a top player goes to a club people focus on him and his success. But I think it's a club vision, a club objective. It's about us.

"[I've had] two decades of big clubs, big challenges and big expectations. I am guilty of it because I create so many expectations, or I went to a club that grew in such a direction that they were waiting for better days. We have to go together and think of the good things we can do."

Having been perceived as Mr Chelsea, joining Spurs would have been harder to take for Chelsea supporters than when he became Manchester United manager. However his appointment still didn't sit comfortably with some Spurs fans, although the vast majority were intrigued by whether he could take them to the next stage and actually win trophies.

Most observers proclaimed that 'The Grumpy One' he became at Manchester United and had actually smiled a lot and cracked a few jokes. The one about the pyjamas of his new club provoked a lovely Guardian Headline: 'The Special Onesie'. In typical flamboyant fashion he announced that his commitment would be clear as he would 'wear the pyjamas of the club' as he responded: "I wear the pyjama of the club, I even sleep in the pyjama of the club, I work and I sleep, and confuse the track suit with the pyjama. So that's the way I am, a club man.

"They have to see me as Mr Porto, Mr Inter Milan and Mr Real Madrid. I am a club man, but a man of many clubs. I am whatever club I am at. I wear the pyjamas of the club and sleep in them. I am a club man, but I am a many club man. I want to have this adventure, go through many countries, going through the Grand Slam of England, Spain and Italy.

"England is the football country which is the best, the most enjoyable. It is normal that managers change clubs. I would not be surprised if Mauricio Pochettino is a manager somewhere else in the Premier League. That is modernity. But, when I come up against one of my old clubs, I only have one club. I am not Manchester United, or Chelsea, or Real Madrid. I am all of them. At each, I give everything. And that is what I will do here."

Mourinho had slept overnight at the training ground and was happy to point out that the facilities had "great beds, huge pillows, huge pillows, amazing". He elaborated, which, of course, was unnecessary, but he was clearly enjoying himself. "I slept in the middle of five or six soft pillows, very, very good, expensive velvet, expensive velvet, so, so good."

Again his past comments didn't appear to fit with what he was prepared to put up with to take the Spurs job. Mourinho had to contend with a documentary film crew following his every move, as Spurs were the latest subject of Amazon's "All Or Nothing" series. Yet the previous year he stated vehemently that allowing behind-the-scenes access at a football club was not to his liking. "You can have a fantastic movie while respecting others," he said when United manager taking aim at City. "You don't need to be disrespectful to have a fantastic movie. You can be a rich club and buy the best players in the world but you cannot buy class and they showed that clearly, that was really obvious."

In a previous edition of All or Nothing, which followed NFL side St Louis Rams in the 2016 season, head coach Jeff Fisher was sacked during the campaign. Amazon actually filmed the meeting in which he was dismissed. At least that didn't happen with Pochettino. Amazon, though, we're at Spurs' training ground to film the arrival of Mourinho at 6.30am on the Wednesday morning.

Mourinho added: "The second reaction is because I am in the movie I could ask for some royalties. But if they send me one of the shirts they had in the tunnel when we played there, the shirts that were saying 'we did it on derby day.' If they send me one of these shirts, I give up about the royalties."

Amazon, though, couldn't have been more pleased with the events that were sure to make compelling viewing.....

Jose set a new club record straight away with media requests for his first press conference. As the debate raged among media, pundits and fans alike whether he was still The Special One or a fading genius, he remained pure box office as Spurs struggled to accommodate the vast army of media wanting to attending his inaugural press conference. As well as the inevitable grilling about his previous remarks about Spurs, one of the first questions he was asked was about Pochettino's departure.

He said: "He knows he gave everything and he leaves with a sad feeling but knowing that he did great work. He will always be welcome here. I have to congratulate him for the work he has done. This club will always be his home. This training ground will always be his training ground. The door will always be open for him. He can come when he wants. When he misses the players, when he misses the people he worked with. The door is always open for him. He will find happiness again. He will find a great club again. He will have a great future.

"I'm not smiling because we have a game in two days and it's not much time. But deep inside I'm really happy and every minute I spend here I realise my decision [to come here] was correct. It's a great club with a great organisation and structure. I'm looking forward to coaching the players and the team and not worrying about things about me. It's not about the structure, it's about the dynamic of the structure.

"I told the players that one of the reasons I decided to come was them. I tried to buy some of them for different clubs and couldn't, some of them I didn't even try because it was impossible. I am not just saying that now, I have said for years. I want to respect the base of work that they have done for five years, it is an update not a change. I am here to try and understand why the results in the last year in the Premier League were not good. I am not here to make dramatic changes and create confusion in their brains. I am going to be very careful."

Mourinho's response was prompted by being pushed by questions such as whether he wanted the perfect "Christmas gift" in the shape of Sporting Lisbon's Bruno Fernandes, a long standing target of his predecessors. He responded, "The best gift for me. I don't need players. I am happy with the ones I have. I just need more time with them. I know them well from playing against them, but you never know them well enough."

The previous manager had run into issues with out of contract experienced and influential players, so he had a major problem there. He commented: "It's early days. I have had no time for individual cases, I don't know how I can try to influence them. The first thing is for the players to feel good, and if they are going to leave in January, or June, or sign a new contract, it has to be based on feeling good. Feeling good is being available on Saturday and being ready for the game. It's about the club and fundamentally you have to be happy, you have to choose what makes you happy.

In the short term we have to try to get two results in the next two matches. In the Premier League we have to disappear from an area we don't belong. Then in the Champions League we have two games to qualify and if we qualify in the first match it will be better."

He fully appreciated picking up the reigns in mid-season poses its own peculiar problems and issues, as he explained: "The difficulty of the job? Every time that a club changes mid-season it is because the situation is not good. It is not easy. But the potential of the club is great and the potential of the players is huge, I am so, so happy. I potentially have a great job in my hands. I have to be balanced. I cannot change things in four days. I have not had a lot of experience of taking teams in the middle of the season, I think I have done it once before with Porto. But I have thought about it a lot and I have to trust the base that is already here. It is not about my fingerprint or myself, it is about stability to provide some comfort to the boys. Let's see."

He portrayed himself as The Humble One! Even confessing that he had made mistakes and admitting that he might make more mistakes, but definitely not the same ones! Asked if he was new and improved after his time out of management, he responded, "I believe so. I always thought the 11 months wasn't a waste of time - I was to think, to analyse, to prepare, to anticipate things. You never lose your DNA, your identity, you are what you are, the good things and bad. Don't ask me what the mistakes are but I realised I made mistakes and I'm not going to make the same mistakes. I'll make new mistakes but not the same. I'm relaxed, motivated and ready, and I think the players have felt that in the two days. This is about Tottenham, it's not about me. You go through periods in life and in this period it's not about me - it's about the club, the players and the fans, and I'm here to help them.

"I am humble, humble enough to try and analysis my career - not just the last year, but the whole thing; the evolution, the problems and the solutions. Not to blame anyone else. It was a great thing. I went really deep with that analysis. A break was very positive for me. It was the first summer I did not work and I felt a little bit at a loss during that pre-season. I was always humble, in my way. The problem is you didn't understand that."

Mourinho's time at United had ended in acrimony; they had just lost 3-1 at Anfield to leave the Old Trafford club 19 points behind leaders Liverpool and he was in constant conflict with Paul Pogba, a man he broke the world record transfer fee to sign from Juventus for £89m in 2016. Yet his team was criticised by United fans for dull, defensive football, contrary to the DNA at Old Trafford and his departure continued his run of having never completed four consecutive seasons in charge of a club.

Asked whether he had been in contact with Real Madrid, Jose said, "If you want to call my friends at Real Madrid, I have so many friends there. The first is the president, he loves me and I love him. I am very proud to leave behind those human relationships. We are friends, we speak, we exchange SMS, we wish luck, we say Merry Christmas, Happy Birthday, good luck in the game. I loved my period there. We did amazing things. We had our problems. We had our frustrations. It was an amazing period for me. I feel always very flattered when I leave these things behind me which go above success, above football. It's about the human being. It's about relations. So Real Madrid is part of my livelihood, part of my life and I always wish them well, I am always happy when Madrid goes in the right direction. If we play them in the Champions League, apart from that match I just want Real Madrid to win and to be successful.

"Yesterday I got 50 text messages from people from Manchester United, from people all over the club. Some players, some staff over different areas of the club, the board, everybody and that for me means the world. That is the most important thing after the medals and trophies. It's not about winning or not winning. It's about the respect people have for you because you were a professional and a good person and you create empathies.'

He was asked whether succumbing to defeat in the Champions League final had taken its toll and eventually cost Pochettino his job. "I don't know because I've never lost a Champions League final but I can imagine it's not easy. You reach one of the biggest moments you can achieve and you cannot do it. But Liverpool. One year they lost the Premier League by one point and the Champions League. Then the following season they're very strong in the Premier League and the season after they lost the Champions League final they won it."

Was he planning a revolution in Spurs playing style? "Very similar, that's what I keep saying. I will try to add some details and sometimes they can make the difference. Progressively we'll arrive to a fingerprint but the style of play should always be adapted – not to the club but to the players' qualities. I read something about Kobe Bryant, a serial winner and a top professional. He says 'people say I'm difficult but I'm only difficult for the ones who don't share my principles'. With me everything's about the team, it's about the group, professionalism, respect for each other, the club and the fans. I cannot run away from this. If there's someone who doesn't share these principles then we have a problem because this is the way I think football should be. To be a big player they have to make others better."

After just two training sessions, he said: 'You will have to ask them if they enjoyed it as much as I did, because I really enjoyed it," he told Tottenham's official website. "That's not just because I was missing training sessions, it was because I really enjoyed it. Of course, there were some limitations. Even today, we didn't have a full group training, still a couple to arrive, so not perfect, but I really enjoyed it and I think the answer was good."

On his main target for the rest of the season he said, "To smile again is very important. In relation to the Premier League, we know where we are, and we know that we don't belong there. We are closer to the bottom than we are to the top, but we have no fear, we are not afraid of that. There is no fear in relation to that. If you think about the distances, we lose motivation, we lose self-esteem, so I don't think we should do that. I think we should just play match after match, the next match we want to win and that's the same about the next and the next and the next until the last. At the end of the season, we will see where we are, but I know we are going to be in a different position than we are now. Let's see what we can do."

Asked by a reporter whether he had got his 'mojo' back, he grinned: "I will have to go to Google translator, but I understand more or less the feeling what you mean. When I don't win I cannot be happy and I cannot change that. That is my DNA. I hope I can influence my players, not to be happy losing football matches it is very hard to be a winner. I want to change that in my players. Sometimes you have to work with people you don't love and work well. I have principles that I cannot change and one of those is that I don't think I can change."

When a familiar face asked a question he responded, "I'm going to meet you every time after the game? In cold tunnels after games, freezing, all the time? Yes it could be worse. You are a good guy". Another reporter he described as a "philosopher" who was bound to ask complicated philosophical questions and he wasn't to be disappointed.

Over in East London, his first opponents West Ham were also quick off the mark with their media team highlighting Mourinho's defeats against the Hammers as he prepared for his Spurs debut at London Stadium. West Ham's official account posted highlights of when their side defeated Chelsea and United coached by Mourinho along with the caption "See you on Saturday, Jose" accompanied by a wink emoji. Included in the video reel was the moment when Mourinho was sent to the stands at Upton Park during a 2-1 defeat for Chelsea in 2015, although the post was quickly deleted.

They also included Mourinho's comments about West Ham following a goalless draw at Stamford Bridge when he criticised the Hammers for playing "19th Century football" under Sam Allardyce. His last visit to West Ham had seen United lose 3-1 with Felipe Anderson and Marko Arnautovic among the scorers. Mourinho had a largely successful record against West Ham in the Premier League. He had faced them 14 times with Mourinho nine wins, three draws and losing twice.

Former Manchester United midfielder Darren Fletcher believed Spurs would see a different Mourinho to the one towards the end of his reign at Old Trafford. Fletcher told BBC Radio 5

Live: "I know for a fact when he left Manchester United he did a little bit of reflecting and asked a few people 'tell me what I was like, give it to me straight'. That, for me, is the sign of someone who had maybe realised he had gone a bit too far in that way. I am sure he had his own frustrations just as the players and people had with him and the things that went on towards the end but I don't expect it to be the Jose we have seen in the last couple of years. I think the Jose that had been affected by Real Madrid and his almost resentment of players, which was different to when he was at Porto, Chelsea and Inter Milan, when he was a players' manager: 'Us against the world'. We've not seen that for a while. You could see towards the end from both points of view, but the fact that he was asking people for an honest opinion of what he was like says to me that it's someone who is reflecting. A little bit of a rest and a bit of reflection, I think we'll see a different Jose Mourinho. I don't know whether it will be the Jose of old but I don't expect it to be the Jose we have seen for the last couple of years."

Mourinho gave a passionate opening address to his new players immediately after being appointed, according to Portuguese outlet *Record* who provided insight into Mourinho's speech to his players, where he vowed to 'be your father, friend, girlfriend, whatever you want,' in a bid to turn their poor form around.

Mourinho took charge of a limited amount of training sessions in the build up to his opening game in what was only his second managerial job where he has arrived mid-season. He was reportedly keen to stress to the group that they were far superior than their position suggested and the reality of their poor start head would be motivation. Mourinho also spoke individually with a number of key figures such as injured goalkeeper Hugo Lloris, striker Harry Kane, Toby Alderweireld, Harry Winks, Eric Dier and Dele Alli.

He was jokingly reminded by his new players about his outspoken statement in 2015 that he would never manage the club due to his affection for Chelsea. He accepted that times had changed and was trying to instil a 'family' mentality within the group.

Old Trafford executive vice-chairman Ed Woodward was one

of the first to call Mourinho even though the United CEO had sacked him just 11 months earlier amid a toxic atmosphere and a dreadful run of form at Old Trafford. Mourinho said, "Maybe I get the opportunity to apologise for not answering 500 (phone calls) of them that I couldn't answer. I have 700 but only had time to answer 200. But it was curious to see, from my last club, so many people showing me that respect, empathy and feeling. It was nice. All of them were special. The first one was from (United managing director) Richard Arnold. The third, fourth or fifth was Ed Woodward. And they were my bosses."

The relationship between Woodward and Mourinho always seemed strained to say the least. Mourinho, however, thinks his relationship with Levy will be much more civil. "Yes, I think we will get on well. He explained to me the vision for the club and I embraced that. It was one of the most important reasons I accepted. So when I did that, it's a very good start. I used to be in clubs that fear him. It's true. He's powerful. He's a businessman, but he's a football man. He has big experience, a part of his intelligence overall, he's a football man, he understands football, he understands the industry, he understands the evolution, he's very clever, he's very intelligent, it's great to have him on my side.

"In reality, who is the manager of any football club?" He said. "We are part of a structure. But what I am is the head coach. Nobody will decide which team is going to play. Nobody's going to decide when I'm going to train. Nobody is going to decide when I give a day off. That's my responsibility." These comments were in contrast to complaints during his time at Old Trafford that he was "only the head coach" after several of his transfer target requests were turned down by Woodward and the board.

Instead of politics, Mourinho reiterated his desire for his players to target silverware and a winning mentality. "With the squad we have and the quality of the whole structure of the club, we can have the same ambitions as they have at clubs that are bigger than us. I don't want my players to fear anything. We go for everything against everybody."

In 41 minutes he fielded 23 questions. His eyes widened when asked whether he needs money to succeed, having spent more than any other manager while in charge of some of the biggest and wealthiest clubs in the world. He couldn't believe the question. "I'm a good guy. Come on!" he pleaded, arms outstretched, palms up. "People cannot wish that I fail. If you are a fan of another club, I understand that, but general people? I'm a good guy. Come on! Give me a break. Maybe it's my fault. Maybe it's also the profile of club I normally get. It's like you people say, I always need money to spend with players. It's not me, it's my clubs. It's the profile of the club, it's the profile of the owner, the profile of, let's say, Real Madrid. Certain profile of players." Whatever he had to say would inevitably spawn a catalogue of back page and some front page headlines and it was also certain to provoke a reaction.

Frank Lampard insisted he would never manage Spurs after Chelsea. The Chelsea manager revealed the pair shared a few messages following Mourinho's appointment. "We had a couple of messages to congratulate him on his new role" but he was ready to be quoted on his own vow in ten years time. "I can firmly say no, and you can replay that in 10 years," he said, "it wouldn't happen."

Asked whether Mourinho had disrespected a supporter base who saw him lift three Premier League titles at Stamford Bridge, Lampard said, Jose Mourinho has managed a lot of football clubs over a long career and sometimes that's what happens. So that's his decision and whether fans judge you or not is out of your hands. It's something you take those decisions and you see, but as a professional you have to understand the right to work. But we do also have this tribal instinct in this country where fans react to that, but that remains to be seen." Lampard was a key part of the teams that delivered great success at Chelsea under Mourinho. The appointment of his old boss ensured that Tottenham were back in contention for a top four finish and Champions League football, such is Mourinho's ability. He added, "History and results speak for themselves. The titles he has won at the clubs he has worked at are not shocks because of the work he has put in. He has done it consistently. That's what we measure him by. I think in the Premier League having people of such character and quality as Jose Mourinho is a great thing. I think we all watched his press conference yesterday waiting for the lines and personality.

"When you ask about Pochettino, I have huge respect for him. I met him a few times. I went to Tottenham's training ground when I was doing my badges and he showed me hospitality. He is a classy man."

Ole Gunnar Solskjaer had no fears over his job after Pochettino's sacking despite United previously courting the outgoing Spurs boss. "It doesn't bother me at all. I've got the best job in the world. If you're in a job or out of one as a manager you want this job. It doesn't matter what happens around it. I have to focus on my job here. I speak with Ed and the owners all the time about how we move the club forward. That doesn't change if another club changes a manager. It's good to have Jose back, definitely. For Mauricio it's always sad when one of your colleagues loses his job before Christmas. A good man."

Solskjaer was prepared for the "circus" that accompanied Mourinho's return. "Jose coming back is going to be a spectacle," said the Norwegian. He had an inkling of what was coming when he saw a television broadcast before Friday's news conference to preview Sunday's trip to Sheffield United, where it was made clear journalists would be asking about Mourinho, and the availability of Pochettino. Solskjaer tried to take command of the situation before he was even asked a question. "Sorry to disappoint you but it is not going to be about Jose or Mauricio," he said. Nevertheless, three of Solskjaer's first six answers were about those two, with a further question at the end about midfielder Nemanja Matic liking a social media post which suggested a further reunion with Mourinho - who bought the Serbian when he was in charge at Chelsea and again when he moved to United. "It's good to have Jose back, especially for you guys," said Solskjaer. "Maybe for me as well because you can talk and write about everything else."

Tottenham's would visit Old Trafford on 4 December. In recent games Jose's name had been sung from the terraces in honour of their former manager in the Sky Sports studios.

MOURINHO'S SPURS DEBUT

One of the mysteries of Spurs' slide from Champions League finalists to also-rans in the Premier League was the massive dip in form of Dele Alli, who had lost his place in the England team, lost his way as one of the country's most dynamic young goalscoring midfielders. One of Mourinho's priorities was to work closely with the 23-year-old to attempt to rekindle the spark that took him from lowly MK Dons to goalscoring Premier League sensation in a matter of months. The conversation between Alli and his new boss inevitably made headline news, virtually everywhere!

Mourinho revealed he asked Alli: "Are you Dele or Dele's brother?"

He replied: "I am Dele."

Mourinho told him: "Okay, so play like Dele."

Mourinho knew Alli has the potential to once again become the top class player he once was, but had completely lost that edge to his game.

Mourinho said: "I already spoke with him. I think he is potentially a fantastic player!"

Mourinho is a coach who can bring some players to their peak. He needs to devise a tactical solution to bring the best out of Alli, as he observed: "Now I have to try to create a tactical situation that he is happy with. I have to give him the right dynamic, prepare him physically well – because he had important injuries too and he's not on the top of his form. On Saturday, if he plays, I can't expect him to go there and be man of the match, but to go through a process that can bring the real Dele back because the real Dele is the one that has impressed us in the past.'

Lucas Moura had started only seven games in seven months since his incredible hat-trick in the Champions League semi-final at Ajax. "When Lucas was at Sao Paulo, before he moved to Paris Saint-Germain, I tried to get him to Real Madrid," said Mourinho. "I met his mum and dad, met with his agent, we spoke in Madrid but PSG came in and we didn't get him. There are others recently and some others who we don't even think about buying because we know it is impossible. So you just admire the player, wish to have him, but forget about it."

If Moura was coveted by the big clubs, how about the England captain? His future had been a source of speculation for some time now. Harry Kane's future was at the top of the agenda with Mourinho. Never before had it become more enticing for Kane to move away from his beloved Spurs in search of glory and even greater riches at a much bigger club. Would that change with the arrival of Mourinho? Antonio Conte wanted Kane when in charge at Chelsea. "He was wasting his time," said Mourinho, "as managers we must have this feeling of what is possible and what is not. When you try to buy Kane it's just an impossible mission."

Mourinho was throwing out a compliment to his new chairman. No one relishes the call to Levy to ask for one of his stars. "I used to be in clubs that fear him," said Mourinho, "It's great to have him on my side." Time would tell, if that proves to be true!

Much would depend on Kane's attitude and in turn much will depend on how Mourinho can galvanise the team around the free scoring striker, who had been in the goals for his country, but not as much as he would like for his club. Mourinho immediately threw out his press conference mantra: "This is not about me!" He went on, "This is about Mr Levy and the club. He has a vision and part of that is to make the club better and bigger. There is no better and bigger club without a better and bigger team. So, to keep the best players is obviously part of that plan. It was not like a promise to me. It was part of his explanation about his vision. Without being specific about players he told me he does not sell players when the manager doesn't want to sell."

Mourinho has no qualms of taking on the biggest egos, the toughest superstars as he coached Cristiano Ronaldo, Didier Drogba, Samuel Eto'o and Zlatan Ibrahimovic. He relishes having a prolific striker, irrespective of how hard they might be to handle. Of Kane he enthuses, "He's one of the best strikers in the world. He's one of the best strikers in the world, no doubt, no doubt. He just needs his team with him, if his team is England or Tottenham, to bring him or to go with him to the next level. And what is the next level? Titles. I think he needs to win with us, with England, he needs to bring something to highlight the quality that he has as a player, the goals he scores, what he brings to the team. He is a top striker and I've worked with some of the top ones."

Mourinho talked of 'small tweaks' not wholesale change, yet there had been so many unanswered questions about why so many players, and virtually every compartment of the team had been malfunctioning. "I'm not going to try to be Einstein," said Mourinho, "I'm going to try to make the players play the way I want. Offensive football but winning matches. Not offensive football and don't win a match for 10 or 11 months. But, yes, attacking football. You are not going to see Harry Kane playing at left back that is for sure."

Careful to give due credit to the outgoing coach, he seemed to be stepping on egg shells not to offend Pochettino or rubbish his legacy, it was clear that Mourinho knew some of the answers and planned to implement them. However, the reference to not winning in 10 or 11 months, just happened to be the exact time frame since Spurs last won away in the Premier League. That will not have been lost on Mourinho. He doesn't miss much!

The message from the dressing room was that the players were hungry for titles and trophies believed Mourinho might be the man to deliver. No one wanted that success more than Kane and he felt the new manager who's 'been there and done that' can deliver what he wanted to ensure that there was no doubt in his mind about staying at the club.

Speaking about the new manager he said: "He's won at every club he's been at. I'm at that stage of my career where I want to win. The manager now coming in, who's been there and done that, it will give us a boost and even more confidence and that's definitely our aim this year. Whenever a new manager comes in everyone wants to impress, everyone has got loads of energy. He made it clear from the day he came in he's an honest manager, he likes to win, his full focus is on Saturdays."

Kane that "it was a bit of a shock" to see Pochettino sacked. "On the night it happened, it was difficult at the time. It is what it is, it's the first time it's happened to me in my career. It's football. Me and Mauricio will hopefully keep a great relationship as friends and continue to talk."

Mourinho was pictured strolling around Chelsea where he lives, in a full Spurs tracksuit complete with navy gilet, a small suitcase in his left hand. He took time out to sign a shirt for a fan, he must have been the only Spurs supporter in west London!

In an introductory video released by Spurs, there seemed a possible dig at his old club Chelsea and United when discussing his desire to bring through young players, something he has been accused of not doing enough of in the past, he said: "There is not one manager in the world that doesn't like to play young players and to help young players to develop – not one. The problem is that sometimes you get into clubs where the work that is below you is not good enough to produce these players. So I look to our history and you see that the academy is always giving talents the first team need. Of course I always look forward to working with that profile." Clearly Frank Lampard had no choice but to turn to the kids with the club under a FIFA transfer ban. But whatever Mourinho had to say after 11 months out of the game was sweet music to the ears of the media, eager to interpret the way they wish, generating even more headlines along the way.

Spurs supporters were warned that Mourinho's guaranteed trophy successes came at a cost. That's the opinion of West Ham's vastly experienced manager Manuel Pellegrini. The Argentinian won a league title in England at City and he believed Mourinho was capable of ending Spurs' wait for a first prize since that League Cup triumph over a decade ago, having not won the FA Cup since 1991 and the league since 1961.

Mourinho often argued winning trophies brings its own happiness, irrespective of criticism of his often pragmatic approach. Pellegrini observed, "Jose Mourinho, in every league where he works, in Italy, in Spain, here in England, he is a manager that has a lot of titles behind him so he will be a manager who is good for football. After that you must think of what kind of football you want. Of course the philosophy of Pochettino is not the same as the philosophy of Mourinho, but he's just in charge of the team in two days so I don't think he will try to change all properly. We'll see Tottenham play a similar way [on Saturday] with some touches of what Mourinho thinks football is." The last sentence highlighted a personal enmity between the two managers who had a history of bad blood dating back to their rivalry in La Liga when Pellegrini managed Villareal. However the West Ham boss insisted Mourinho was "not my friend, but not my enemy" ahead of facing him in the London derby. Mourinho and Pellegrini had chequered past; Mourinho aimed a dig at him in his time at Real Madrid and they clashed in the Premier League when he was at Chelsea and the Chilean at City. Pellegrini said of Mourinho: "He's not my enemy. Everyone has the option to play football the way they want, to talk how they want to and you can't be criticising always what I think. That's why he's not my friend, but he's not my enemy. We have different ways of thinking about things, that's the only difference we have." Asked whether the 66-year-old will have a drink with Mourinho after the game, he replied: "Maybe. I don't have any problems [with him]. We have been together a lot of times outside of football, and I repeat, he's not my enemy."

He was under pressure after a seven-game winless run in all competitions that included five defeats which had left the Hammers 16th in the table, five points above the relegation zone. Pellegrini targeted "the most important game of the season" to turnaround their season. "I trust the players a lot because I know they can do it as they've demonstrated a lot of times against big teams. I hope that tomorrow, especially in a derby game that for our fans is the most important game of the season, we'll see the West Ham that we saw at the beginning of the season."

WEST HAM UNITED v TOTTENHAM HOTSPUR 23RD NOVEMBER 2019

Mourinho arrived at the London Stadium smiling as he leds his staff and players off the team coach and couldn't stop smiling on his journey to the dressing room. A cameraman, security and some club staff, were the few to witness his arrival as young mascots in West Ham kits lined the passage to the dressing rooms. Mourinho greeted them with some high fives and a familiar cheeky wink and goes back to fist bump one or two he missed. He looked in a very good mood.

An hour later the teams announced; the new manager opted for the same 4-2-3-1 formation that Pochettino successfully favoured in his early days. Eric Dier, once a target for Jose at Man United, was back for a rare outing in midfield, alongside Harry Winks. Alderweireld was the only 'contract rebel' to make the team – Eriksen and Rose were on the bench, Vertonghen is injured. Mourinho made three changes to the side who drew 1-1 at home to Sheffield United in Pochettino's last game. Moura in for injured Ndombele, Winks in for Moussa Sissoko, Alderweireld back as Giovani Lo Celso on the bench.

Jose told BT Sports, "I think today is about a bit of everything. Motivation - I think they always had it. People think when results are bad it's about motivation but they are professionals and they always try their best. Tactics - we have just a few little changes but I have not changed a lot just little things I think will help. Today is important but our future is also very important. We are going to try and find some positions and dynamic which we have had chance to work with Kane, Son and Moura. Today is about finding happiness." On Eriksen being relegated to the bench he says, "I need to understand what is in Christian's mind or heart and we have to make the right decision for the club."

With five minutes to kick off, Mourinho walked out after his team to sit on the away team benches alongside his new number two Joao Sacramento with a scrum of dozens of photographers focused on his every move and within minutes Harry Kane 'scores' but is flagged offside. Mourinho jumps up and out into his technical area for the first time before taking his seat again. A few minutes later and Mourinho is in the technical area, assisting the referee by waving an imaginary flag to suggest a Spurs throw in. Michal Oliver agrees and gives the marginal call to Tottenham. Jose spends the rest of the half prowling across the technical area with hands in pockets

It takes 36 minutes for the first goal of the Mourinho era to arrive: Son is alert to collect a pass from Alli, he skilfully finds a yard and lashes a shot through Roberto. Jose is out of his seat and punching the air with a double fist pump – then gets a hug from his assistant Sacramento, who had been out earlier to suggest a tactical tweak. Six minutes later things went from good to great for Jose, who was on his feet in animated celebration; down on one knee, his fists pumping. Alli was again involved, keeping the ball in near the touchline with a clever flick on, despite being on the floor. Son drives into the box down the left and puts over a superb cross, Lucas Moura slides in to get a toe to the ball ahead of Cresswell to force it home.

In injury time at the end of the first half, Spurs grab a third; Aurier swings over a cross from the right, Kane beats his marker to head past Roberto. Mourinho is laughing. It's the perfect start. Mourinho ignores his players celebrating at one end of the pitch and instead tried to get the attention of keeper Gazzaniga at the other end. The keeper doesn't hear him, so Mourinho calls over Harry Winks to give him lengthy instructions, which Winks relays to his team-mate.

A contented Jose emerges for the second half and it all seems to be plain sailing for Spurs before Harry Kane gets a knock and the physio is called for. Mourinho consults the physio when he returns. Mourinho spoke to Kane briefly before he returned to the field. An apparently serene Spurs defensive performance is broken in the 74th minute when West Hame get a goal following good work from Mark Noble. It's a glimmer of hope for the home fans. Davies is injured, Rose is on as sub. Mourinho high-fives Davies as he walks off. Dele Alli looked to be back to his best but is now replaced by Eriksen, he gets handshake and a pat on the back from Mourinho.

On 86 minutes, Snodgrass and Kane clash close to the technical area. A handful of players square up, Mourinho steps to the edge of the pitch but does not get involved. He had a quiet word with Eriksen over tactics instead. In the closing stages VAR rules out a

Declan Rice heaping more misery on the home support. before Ogbonna scores in the last minute of injury time to make it 3-2 but there is no time for an equaliser.

At the whistle Mourinho shakes hands with Pellegrini and gives Alli a hug before walking out on to the pitch to shake hands with a few West Ham players and the officials. He hugs his players one by one, keeping his distance from those celebrating with the fans at one end. He applauds the fans more than once, and gets a round of applause back from them at the end, as he is the last man off the pitch and down the tunnel.

Having lost his first ever competitive game as manager, with Benfica in September 2000, Mourinho has now gone unbeaten in his first game in charge at each of his eight clubs since, including two different spells with Chelsea. Mourinho won as many points in this game as Pochettino managed in his final 12 away Premier League games (W0 D3 L9).

Mourinho hugged Alli at the final whistle, before sharing a few handshakes with his 'bench'. Afterwards he said, "I was really happy before we conceded the two goals, we were playing well, bringing to the game things we had tried in training. And we had the ball to make it 4-0 and kill the game. We are lucky I have so many years in the Premier League so I told the players at half-time 'even if we are 3-0 in the 85th minute the game will still be open'. But there were also many factors. The emotions of losing the previous manager, people coming back from national teams and fatigue in the last 20 minutes. The most important thing was to win, not matter how. The boys are happy and that's what I really wanted."

As for Alli, he observed, "I'm happy with him, I spent a few minutes with him in training and outside the pitch. And we were saying that the best Dele Alli has to be back. He's too good to not be one of the best players in the world and not playing with the national team. Dele was like the team: he was brilliant for 60-65 minutes, and then he paid also the price and went a little bit down. But I think he was the old Dele Alli. The Dele Alli of a couple of years ago, who impressed not just England but a lot. He did exactly what I wanted him to do after two days of work. I'd tried to make it clear to him exactly the places I wanted him to play, offensively and defensively. He is an intelligent footballer and I am pleased with his performance."

Alli was delighted. His imposter brother had been given the day off! "It's been a very tough week for us emotionally. We've spent a long time with Pochettino and we were very sad but we had a job to do. We had to go out for the fans and try and stay as positive as we can. We have to carry on momentum and keep winning, we need to start that from now. There is still a lot to work on and we need to improve from now on. There's no hiding how much Pochettino meant to the players and in particular me. We did not really change too much [under Mourinho], just a few little tweaks, maybe a few changes in the way we press." As for his own performance he said, "I think I have been performing well so far this season but I need to get better than my old form and get to my best."

Mourinho, though, was at pains to repeat his new mantra: "It's not about me, it's about the players and club. I will hate if somebody say 'Jose made an impact'. I made no impact. Nothing. I just helped them a little bit to win this match. I think the team had 60 amazing minutes, total control, total dominance - using the principle we brought to the training sessions. Then they went a bit down, physically. I'm not blaming the coaching staff they had. I'm blaming the nature of things, national team weeks. Some players only arrived back yesterday."

The win catapulted Tottenham from 14th back to within to challenging distance for the top four, although with much to still do, but enough for Mourinho to describe the emotional wrench of the 11 months out of management. "To confess, the most difficult moments for me was in my mind this summer, when I didn't have a pre-season and was looking at other managers, clubs, teams doing pre-season. The most weird feeling was going to stadia and I was asking myself what I was doing here: here in the box, or the Sky television studios. Today is where I belong. My natural habitat."

After such a long wait for an away win, Mourinho seemed to blame the mood music within the team's dressing room under

Pochettino when he said: "It was very, very important. Months without music in the away dressing room. Without a smile, without happiness, and they did it. I'm very happy with them. They can do what they want with the music. When you go away, the music after the game I like. A victory is something that you have to value. It's hard to win matches. You work hard in these two days. The boys worked hard today. It's something you have to value. You can't just say, "Okay, we won". In the same way if you lose you can't be in a nightclub with your friends in a few hours. When you win you have to feel it. The music was loud. I don't care what music it is. I just like the feeling the boys are happy.

"I think if somebody didn't watch the game and just knew the result, they'd think it was very difficult for us to win. But the feeling is we were closer to 4-0 than West Ham were to 3-1. But this is the Premier League. And I think also my players paid the price of a very, very difficult week. A week where they arrived from their national teams, some of them arrived from difficult matches, and there was a changed manager, a new guy arrives, new training sessions and new ideas, the emotional things that surround that.

"I don't think it's ever easy for a football player to work with a coaching staff one day and, the next, other people are there. It is difficult to process. Physically, the team had a break. Probably also they were a little bit scared of that mental barrier of the bad results away. So the last 20-25 minutes were not easy. But we played very, very well for about an hour. Really well. I'm really happy for the boys."

The joke about his imposter brother was the first thing Mourinho said to Dele Alli after becoming Tottenham manager but he accepted the criticism. "A lot of people have been saying that, so it was nothing new. In that sense, to have it honestly said to your face was nice because a lot of people would prefer to say it behind your back. It didn't shock me. Playing in the Premier League, you expect it when you are not performing - to be criticised. It is just important you listen to the right people. I am my own biggest critic. I know what I need to work on."

Alli felt guilty immediately after Pochettino was sacked. "When it first happened, you just blame yourself when you're sad and you don't really look at the big picture. We've had some amazing journeys together, we grew together - all the coaching staff that were here and the players, we all grew. We achieved a lot in terms of where we came from. We're all very thankful to him. You can't help but feel a bit to blame because we were out there but when I look back I gave 100 per cent and so did all the players. Sometimes it just doesn't work out. The chairman made a decision and, like I say, we owe [Pochettino] a lot of thanks.

"I came here as an 18-year-old and I've been through a lot of ups and downs here but he's helped me through it all. I can't thank him enough. I felt it was important as soon as I saw the news to get in contact. I was very upset but I tried to get in contact with him and the next day I went to see him. It was just a conversation between two friends. I've seen him more than I see my own family in the last five years, so it was very tough. But this is football. But for sure he is someone I'm going to stay in contact with."

Mourinho dismissed rumours claiming he signed Zlatan Ibrahimovic for Tottenham saying it "doesn't make sense" because he has the "best striker in England" in Kane. Ibrahimovic, who played for Mourinho at Inter Milan and Manchester United, was available on a free transfer after his two-year spell at LA Galaxy ended. Mourinho had "more than a connection" with the former Sweden forward he described as an, "Amazing player, amazing guy, but I would say no chance." Mourinho's first game in charge of each club he has managed - were all in the league bar Inter Milan (an Italian Super Cup penalty shoot-out win over Roma) and Manchester United (a Community Shield win over Leicester).

MOURINHO'S FIRST GAME AT THE LANE

Jose Mourinho, who won the Champions League with unfancied Porto and Inter Milan, was sure he would take Tottenham into the knock-out stages by beating Olympiakos in his first home match in charge. Spurs were second in Group B and would qualify by beating the Greek side. "With these boys I will never be afraid of a

Champions League match," said Mourinho.

Tottenham had reached last season's final, losing 2-0 to Liverpool, but made a bad start throwing away a two-goal lead to draw 2-2 away against Olympiakos and losing 7-2 at home to group leaders Bayern Munich. Back-to-back wins over Red Star Belgrade - 5-0 at home and 4-0 away in Serbia - left Spurs needing one more victory to take them into the knock-out phase for a third successive season. Olympiakos were top of the Greek Super League but bottom of Group B with only one point from four games.

"We need to qualify," added Mourinho. "It's only when my teams arrive in the quarter-finals that I start thinking 'we have a chance'. In this moment we are far from it. Every Champions League campaign there are details around your success or failure. How many times I lost on penalties or in the last minute. Details make the difference.

"As for Spurs last season, they had little details for them. VAR [Video Assistant Referee] was with them [against Manchester City], the Lucas [Moura] goal in Amsterdam [against Ajax]. To arrive in the final is an achievement but not history.

"I love the competition as much as everyone in football. Not everyone has the privilege of being a Champions League winner. I have done it two times and would love to add a third. In the case of Spurs last season, just the fact of reaching the final is an amazing achievement, no doubt."

Mourinho's comment about reaching the final not being history summed up how his approach to management differed from his predecessor. Victory is everything, nothing else matters to him, not how you achieve it, whether the critics adore the style or the methods. Winning makes the fans happy, attracts new players and helps you keep your best players. "Sometimes we use words to try to describe things but the words do not reflect precisely what it is," he added, "I would change "miracle"' to "very difficult. I would not use the word 'miracle', although probably I have done that in the past a few times.

"There are some teams with a different culture of victory.

There are clubs and teams with a different potential, experience and know-how. But with these boys, I will never be afraid of any Champions League match that comes into our faces. We need to qualify, that is the focus. I always say that. Not even in the last 16 did I used to think about winning the trophy. Only in the quarter-finals can you do that. It is still far, but in the last eight start thinking we have a chance.

"But, as I was saying, give me time to work, give me time to float my ideas with these boys and I will have no problem at all going to any stadium at all to face any big opponent in Europe or in England. We are not going to be afraid of anybody."

Tottenham were without defender Ben Davies, who had an ankle injury. Mourinho said that the selection of Eriksen - a substitute at West Ham - will be based on a "perspective of the future". Mourinho also had to concentrate on the perceived hangover from the Champions League Final loss to Liverpool in Madrid. "If Mauricio says that [losing the final affected the players] then he's been here and he's sharing his feelings. It's like landing on the moon but you don't do it. Look at Liverpool; they had the frustration of not winning and then the next season they reached the final and won it."

The new manager had a lengthy private chat with Eriksen over his future - and Amazon listened in. "I'm not going to tell you what we said. Just me and him – and Amazon," Mourinho said. "He's committed, loves the club and is one of us."

Eric Dier was already convinced Mourinho would make Spurs winners. He observed: "I think he's the perfect person to have followed on from Pochettino - that's the feeling I have. We're really happy that if someone was to replace Pochettino, it was him. His record is unbelievable and he transmits that confidence. The way he speaks, you believe it, you feel it from him. I think for everyone, we're very lucky to have played under Pochettino and now Mourinho. We couldn't be luckier.

"I think he said to you guys, like he said to us, that he doesn't want to come in and change everything two days before a game. I think it's going to be something gradual that we move towards over time."

Mourinho admitted that he had not yet contacted his predecessor, in the main because it's an emotional time. "I didn't because I know what he is feeling. I have been there and I know that there is a period where the best thing for us sometimes is to process our feelings, to process what happened with us and then in a couple of weeks, two three weeks then we are open to the world.

"We are open again to embrace the different period in our lives, so I want to respect that, to give that feeling to him. But I spoke with his son (Mauricio), who is a player in our youth categories, and I think through his boy he can understand my feelings too.

"Of course I will call him but I want to let him process. I also told the players in contact with him to make him feel completely free to come here any time he wants. If he wants to come to a training session, great, if he wants to come to a dinner in the Lodge with the boys, perfect. If he wants me to be there, I will be, if he just wants it to be him and the boys, let's do it that way. I just want him to feel that this house belongs to him."

Mauricio Pochettino broke his silence on his sacking with a statement released by the League Managers Association, humbly offering his gratitude for being 'part of Tottenham Hotspur's history'. The carefully worded statement via the LMA said: "I would like to thank Joe Lewis and Daniel Levy for giving me the opportunity to be part of Tottenham Hotspur's history. I would like to thank also everyone I met at Tottenham, all the club staff and the football players during these five and a half years. Finally I would like to give a special mention to the fans who make this club so great with their fantastic support. I gave the best of me to accomplish the objectives I was asked for in our first meeting. There were equally tough challenges as exciting success. Best wishes for the future, I am sure we will cross paths again."

Pochettino issued the statement a week after his sacking with speculation rife that he wouldn't be out of the game for long as the futures of Manchester United manager Ole Gunnar Solskjaer and his Arsenal counterpart Unai Emery continued to intensify. Equally, rumours swirled around the club concerning Pochettino final days and weeks in charge, suggestions that he had become distant by the end of his tenure — rarely taking sessions, preferring to watch from inside the training ground canteen. Pochettino had become disengaged and the players knew it by his demeanour. By the end of his reign, Tottenham's Enfield HQ had become a rather miserable place to work, made worse by Pochettino's crankiness, according to sources close to the players, which usually means the players' agents. By contrast it was being suggested that Mourinho's arrival had lightened the mood. He was fully involved in training sessions and the players, in turn, felt his enthusiasm and it was immediately rubbing off on them and the evidence was visible on the field with improved results.

Mourinho shared jokes with his players and staff at their training complex, engaged in regular individual discussions with his players, and his engaging charming personality, at least the one he usually brings to a new club, encouraged a squad who appeared to be going flat in the last throws of Pochettino's time. New assistant head coach Joao Sacramento's sessions were said to be refreshing and engaging, and it always helps when a new manager kicks off a new regime with a winning start.

In his first address to the squad, Mourinho's message was clear. "Believe in me and we'll become winners" and that a top four finish was not out of reach as it had been suggested in the media with such a poor run of recent results under Pochettino. Careful not to disrespect the players' achievements during Pochettino's reign, he was pretty blunt in telling them that glory would finally be theirs if they trusted him and many, led by the captain, were tired of being labelled the 'nearly men' tag and in Mourinho they now had a manager who was a proven winner with more than 20 career titles.

Speaking after the win over Olympiakos, Kane revealed, "It's early days. We have a good relationship so far. We talk, we try to help the team. Obviously, me being one of the leaders in the team, he looks to me for feelings and advice on the team. When you are winning games, it definitely helps your relationship. Hopefully we can build a strong relationship."

ARSENAL? NO WAY JOSE!

Or, at least that how's the new Spurs manager portrayed the speculation that he had been lined up by the Gunners prior to the sacking of Umai Emery. At first Mourinho had refused to discuss interest from Arsenal, insisting that he was 'so happy' at new club Tottenham that he wouldn't even contemplate whether their north London rivals would have wanted him but when the Gunners eventually sacked Emery on Friday morning, speculation that Arsenal wanted Mourinho before he moved to Spurs grew in intensity.

Asked about Arsenal's intentions during his press conference the day before the Bournemouth game, Mourinho deflected any links with Arsenal. "No point in telling you," he said, "I'm so happy here I cannot think of the possibility of another club. If you put any other club in the world in front of me now I'd say 'no'."

However Mourinho knew he had to clarify the situation as the rumour mill was working over time, and it was reported he had met Arsenal's head of football Raul Sanllehi earlier in the month as Emery's position began to come under threat. Asked if there had been any contact with Arsenal, he responded, "No, no. Of course, I never denied, because I never deny things. But when it was written that I was in a meeting with Mr Sanllehi it was not true."

Mourinho insisted his current job was better than his previous roles at Manchester United, Chelsea and Real Madrid. "I'm so happy here that I couldn't even think about the possibility to go to another place. You can put now in front of me any club in the world, I would not move. The facilities in this one are the best I've ever seen and I've been in big clubs. It's not like I arrive here from small clubs and think: 'Wow'. I've been in big, big clubs with very good conditions. Chelsea, very good conditions, United the same, Madrid, the same, Inter the same. It's not like I've been in bad conditions but here it's fantastic. The stadium is brand new and is the best stadium in the world.

"You know how much I like the Premier League, that's the first point. You go back to Porto, my first opportunity to leave my country I had lots of options. It was England. I was in Real Madrid, probably the dream club for the majority of us. I left Real Madrid to come to the Premier League. Now, I stayed in the Premier League which I always say is my natural habitat. So many years I like it a lot. So that is a point.

"The second point is this club. You know what the club is showing me. The vision they have for the future and everything they are as a club in terms of structure, organisation, feelings, a big club but with a concept of a family, working together with people. See them everyday. Everybody is around me. Mr Levy is next door to me, his office is next door to me. Everyday I need him he is there. He needs me, I'm there. Then the chief scout (is) the next door. I meet him every day. If I want to speak he's there. If he wants to speak with me, I'm here. The academy boss three doors (down). Everything is close. We arrive here early in the morning, we leave late in the afternoon. I like very much this kind of empathy and the way we are working. And, again, very, very important, I like the players. Very important."

In the middle of a managerial merry-go-round Mauricio Pochettino was among the names linked with replacing Emery, but Mourinho was already looking forward to playing against Arsenal again - whoever was in charge. The Gunners were due at Tottenham Hotspur Stadium in late April. "I look forward to playing against Arsenal. I want to play against Arsenal. I know what it means for our fans," Mourinho said. "But with Mauricio or Emery or Freddie Ljungberg or whoever else, that's no problem. I know the big ones and I know that's a big one. Not just because Arsenal is a big club that fights for the same objectives as we do. But also I know the meaning. And I like it.

"I never played against Pochettino in my life. Never. Man United against Tottenham, yes. Tottenham against Chelsea, yes. But never me against Pochettino. So if he goes to Arsenal or if he goes to, I don't know which club, it will never be me against him. It will be me against his club."

Arsenal were in the middle of their worst run of form for 27 years, and had they acted just a few weeks earlier it was suggested they would have tried to appoint Mourinho while he remained out of work. Other names linked with the Arsenal hot-seat were Pochettino, Carlo Ancelotti, Max Allegri, and Nuno Espirito Santo but it was thought Pochettino was awaiting his appointment at Old Trafford.

The rumours refused to go away, with one report that Mourinho had been offered £12million by Real Madrid to reject a top job in football to wait for Zinedine Zidane to depart. Mourinho had been linked for months with a return to the Spanish giants initially suffering a shaky start in La Liga. Zidane ended up staying after a turnaround in form. Reports in Spain claimed that many of the team were against his return; Mourinho managed Los Blancos from 2010 to 2013, when he fell out with a number of players. Borussia Dortmund, AC Milan, Lyon and Chinese Super League outfits had all been linked to Spurs new boss.

Mourinho tried to focus on his first Premier League game in front of the home fans, who had hitherto been muted in their response to his arrival to replace the popular Pochettino.

Back at the new Lane, Spurs found a new momentum as they romped into a three goal lead against Bournemouth, as one fan tweeted that if Mourinho got them into the top four from where he started and also won the FA Cup, then Pochettino would be a distant memory! Alli got the first two and looked back to his best, re-energised under the new manager, and with the third from Sissoko, Spurs had their mo-jo back, or should it be Mou-jo? That was Sissoko's first Premier League goal in 69 appearances! What has Mourinho put in their drinking water? As if to emphasis that it's not going to be so easy, but promises to be highly entertaining, Bournemouth got one back with a wonderful free-kick from Harry Wilson, on loan from Liverpool, and then in the sixth minute of six minutes of injury time Wilson got a second, leaving Spurs hanging on at the end of added on time to added on time.

It seems Mourinho is specialising in 3-2's! But three straight wins was not a bad start!

Mourinho started to look at home with his new club. He gave a fist bump to the lucky Tottenham ball boy as he celebrated the opening goal, he stretched out his fist to greet his 'new mate'! The ball boy had been invited to meet the players at the pre-match meal. Callum Hynes met Kane and the Spurs squad and joined them for their pre-match meal at the stadium. Afterwards Mourinho said it was, 'Happy days for the kid and hopefully we gave him amazing memories for the rest of his life, so beautiful for him,' said Mourinho, who said he was now considering inviting one of the ball-boys into the pre-match meal ahead of every home game.

The fans had taken to Mourinho and started to believe in him. Mourinho commented: "The fans love the club, I'm not saying they love me but they accept me as a top professional who wants to give everything for the club. People have more reasons to love me if they like my work, but the fans are behind the team and the see us working hard to get to a position in the table that is more suitable to the talent of this squad."

Spurs back-to-back league wins put them right on the heels of Chelsea, as Mourinho remarked: "When I arrived we were 12 points behind the Champions League last position. I said I didn't want to think about it. We were eight or nine from a Europa League position. If you think about it you get depressed, not playing European football next season. So don't think about it. Now we are closer and we have match, match, match for the Christmas period. We have a lot to improve on and we need to keep working. You have the chance to break down, we have the chance to put pressure on the opponent."

The next few games would see Mourinho come up against old friends, firstly at Old Trafford before the Chelsea game, the team in Mourinho's sights as he chased that fourth Champions League spot. "We play Chelsea at the end of December, if the game was tomorrow, we would play them with six points difference, it would be a fantastic situation to play them. But we play them in the end of December. We have to keep close, as close as possible. But we have a lot to work and a lot to improve."

Spurs were at least back in the race for another top-four finish, something that looked highly unlikely until Mourinho replaced Pochettino. Mourinho took a reignited Spurs from 14th up to fifth, and hoped the forthcoming hectic schedule can see them continue their march up the table.

SLAPPED DOWN BY OLE

Jose Mourinho suffered on his return to Old Trafford. He suffered a kick in the knee during the game, he suffered a Rashford double, he suffered a dent to his ego at losing and he suffered a derogatory pat on the head by his rival Ole Gunnar Solskjaer.

United fans were in hysterics after Solskjaer patted Mourinho on the head "like a puppy" as the managers exchanged the usual polite after match handshake. It had all been very convivial between Mourinho and the man who took his job apart from a very mild barbed pre match comment but it kicked off at the full-time whistle when the pair hugged and shook hands on the touchline at the end, as Solskjaer could not resist patting him patronisingly on the head. One United fan tweeted: "Never thought I'd see the day Ole would take Mourinho's job and then pat his head like a puppy after beating him." Another posted: "Delighted for Ole that he got a chance to give Mourinho the final patronising pat on the head after shaking hands. Fair play." A fellow user: "Ole dropping the dismissive head pat on Mourinho akin to dropping a stone cold stunner on Steve Austin." Mourinho apparently retaliated by planting his hand on the Norwegian's head in the tunnel afterwards, although there was no video footage to collaborate it.

Asked about the 'head pat' incident afterwards Mourinho played it down, saying: "No one likes to lose the game. But we are all the same, we just want to win games."

It wasn't the only injury Mourinho suffered as he grimaced in pain and clutched his knee after United winger Daniel James crashed into him following a Harry Wins' tackle after 13 minutes.

Mourinho's entrance had been perfect. An 18-second clip on Spurs Twitter account showed their new manager embracing six different United employees as he made his way in; security guards, stewards, photographers, near enough everyone he recognised from his time at Old Trafford as he made his way through the tunnel, got a hug or a handshake as he progressed to the visitors dressing room, the one he ordered to be reduced in size so he could make the home dressing room bigger. There was already a bit of noise inside Old Trafford when Mourinho emerged first in his big black coat, for more hugs, this time with goalkeepers David De Gea and Sergio Romero who were waiting to warm up.

"It's good, I shook hands happily they are all good people, nice people here. Now it's time to go to work. They want to win and I want to win and they will have the same objective."

He made his way down the tunnel to pitch side where he received warm applause and a song for Solskjaer from the United fans, as the two managers exchanged a big handshake in front of the technical area as soon as Solskjaer arrived.

Yet an early goal from Marcus Rashford set the tone for the evening. Jesse Lingard was under pressure from Sanchez but got the ball to Rashford, whose long range speculative shot from a tight angle should not have beaten Gazzaniga at his near post. It bounced, the keeper got his hand to it but could only push it onto the post on the way in – a goalkeeping error. That made five goals and four assists in his past 11 league games for a striker Mourinho had often played as an auxiliary full back during his time at United.

Mourinho returned to the dug-out when Rashford scored but he was quickly back out on the touchline to encourage his team with some forceful applause before he United's Welsh winger James collided painfully with his knee. And it wasn't just the Spurs boss who had to weather the storm as Rashford twice went close to doubling United's lead, first with a thunderous shot from distance that the keeper got a faint touch to as it rattled the underside of the bar before a curler saw the keeper stretch to turn it away, Gazzaniga made a string of saves to keep Spurs in it.

Against the run of play a dangerous Spurs attack just before half time provided them with a way back in the game. Aurier's angled volley was saved by De Gea's legs at the near post, the ball spun up and Alli plucked it out of the air, swivelled and finished for one of the season's great goals. What an equaliser! Alli looks even better than his previous best under Mourinho! That made four goals in four games since the new boss had arrived, even if it took a long check by VAR to give the goal as the ball appeared to brush his arm. Commentator Glenn Hoddle was impressed, "super, super goal" said Hoddle, one of the few Spurs players of the past capable of such delicate skill.

Yet Spurs were caught cold straight after the break. On 48 minutes Marcus Rashford skinned Aurrier and raced into the box, Sissoko chased back and tried to get a toe to the ball but stood on the Mancunian's toe instead - penalty. The United youth product had to wait an age to convert the spot kick before calmly slotting it to Gazzaniga's left.

Most in the home crowd expected a Spurs assault in what remained of the game as United continued to squander possession and chances but aside from a Dele Alli shot that was well saved towards the end, Tottenham produced little of note.

Mourinho was realistic in his assessment of the game, "We didn't play well for 30 minutes, then I thought we did. We can't concede a goal like the second goal. It was a throw-in, everyone was sleeping, they only reacted when Marcus Rashford got near the box. Once he is inside the box it's more difficult to defend and he was clever and waited for the touch."

VAR confirmed Sissoko tripped Rashford. Mourinho added: "I didn't see it, but I think what happened inside of the box is a consequence of what happened before. I think when Ashley Young had the ball we have to be alert immediately, we were not, we gave space to Rashford to receive the ball, it was only when he received the ball that we woke up. He was dangerous and I knew that. I gave the players the best possible information about it. The first is a typical Rashford goal, coming inside and shooting. Also the way he attacked the defenders with his second goal. Our boys knew it, they knew it clearly.

"United were more aggressive in the first 30 minutes, more intense, so they deserve to win. I knew United at home would use the crowd, they've got a lot of young players and I knew they'd want to press and play with intensity, I told my players, but they couldn't react."

With an intense period of Christmas games on the horizon, Mourinho knew the areas he needed to work on. "I know that this team needs to be more aggressive. We need to win more duels, we need to start the game with more intensity. We need to make the opponent feel what United made us feel. You need to make opponents feel like they're going to be in trouble. We were reactive rather than proactive."

But Mourinho paid United a back-handed compliment saying, "United's results against the best teams this season have been good. Chelsea, Liverpool, Leicester. For the way they play it is easier for them. They are not afraid to have a defensive approach. It is easier for them against better teams, against teams who want more of the ball." United had 46% possession but more shots and more shots on target.

Dele Alli continued his rich vein of form since the manager's arrival and Mourinho observed: "Dele is fine, he gave a good performance and tried everything, even in the second half when it's more difficult and they are more compact."

With a touch of the old Mourinho he accused the Red Devils of milking injuries to see out the game. "We started bad, they started well. They scored the first goal, could have scored the second and for the first 30 minutes they were not just better than us, they were much better than us. For the last 15 minutes, the story was different. I thought the second half we'd be back to normality and normality was to have control of the game but when you concede a goal like we did it's difficult. They took a few steps back, started to block low and they were clever in the way they were getting fouls and pretending injuries and controlling and then still dangerous on the counter-attack.

"We were punished by our mistake for the second goal. The reason I want to say clearly they deserved to win the game was because in the first 30 minutes of the game they were much better than us. It was not just today, if you look to our previous matches it was the same. Against Olympiakos we didn't start well, against Bournemouth it took time, rather than being proactive we are a little bit more reactive."

Mourinho won't take much from his first game back at Old Trafford in terms of his team's performance, and there won't be any Amazon video footage in the dressing room as United put a stop to that just as they stopped Manchester City filming for their documentary two seasons ago. United moved a point ahead of Jose's new club in the table into the top six, but, at least Jose enjoyed his reception – "It was nice, polite, educated and what I was expecting."

Mourinho spent the night at the training ground after the Old Trafford defeat but was back at work at 8am, and demanding his new charges were "raging" whenever they experience defeat, rather than "sad". He detected sadness in the dressing room rather than anger and, as his team attempt to bounce back against Burnley, he wanted their mentality needs to change.

"One of the things I said was that I saw a sad dressing room, a sad plane and that's not what I like after a defeat. You have to be more than that. You have to be raging, angry, not sad. Being sad will not resolve your problems. You need that mentality. We have to play and resolve the problems step by step. We have problems, there is no doubt, but we have players with quality, a great human dressing room. But we have to change the feeling of being sorry. We need to be more than that.

"The thing I want from them and I hope they understand my message, is that I don't like sad people in this sense of the word. I don't want people to be sad after the game. I want people who, after defeat, would love a match the next morning. Not feeling sad. Sad is not the kind of reaction that I like and these players need this kind of message. They need to say: 'OK, I don't accept defeat, that is not something that belongs to my culture. I don't accept defeat.' Don't be sad. Let's go – next day, next match."

Mourinho had had little time so far to fine-tune his ideas in training but planned to work with his players as he could see some days now available to get to grips more with his own ideas. "Probably in normal conditions it would be nice for the players to have some days off, but it is the kind of week where it is my only chance to have them, so we are going to work that week."

Christian Eriksen's future remained unresolved, Mourinho said the pair had spoken but would not reveal the outcome of those talks. "It's for him to say. I have to defend the best interests of my club. I will not tell you what we said. I am perfectly fine if he wants to say but I have to have respect for the player."

But certain players were suddenly thriving. Ivory Coast defender Serge Aurier believed Mourinho had lifted spirits and helped turn around the team's fortunes. "We are happy, he is a great manager, he wins everywhere. He won many trophies but I think everyone needs to give their best. We didn't start this season in a good way like last season. When we don't win its not the same, now we are winning so its good. We need to maintain that and fight for top four in order to qualify for champions league next season." Aurier had started all the games under Mourinho, scoring agaisnt Olympiakos. "This is the best moment for me, I need to play and I am happy because I am playing game by game," said Ivory Coast national team captain.

Moiurinho got the response he was after with a thrashing of Burnley that warmed the hearts of Spurs fans, and endeared him to the new manager. Mourinho dubbed Son Heung-min "Sonaldo", and compared him to former Brazil striker Ronaldo, after the South Korean raced from one box to the other for a stunning solo run reminscent, one commentator claimed, of Diego Maradona's goal against England in 1986. Yet for the manager he was reminded of the original Ronlado as Son collected the undisputed Goal-of-the-Season title during Spurs 5-0 win. It was a big three points for Spurs in their race to finish in the top-four particurely as in-form Chelsea surprisingly lost at Everton in the earlier kick-off on

Saturday.

Kane fired a brace, with a Lucas Moura tap-in and Moussa Sissoko finished off a slick move after a 'wall' pace from Kane as Mourinho's men shone at the Tottenham Hotspur Stadium in a perfect resposne to their defeat at Old Trafford.

Mourinho likened Son's wonder goal to Ronaldo's mazy effort for Barcelona against Compostela in 1996, before praising the 27-year-old's work ethic. "Even before this goal my son calls him Sonaldo, and today he was Sonaldo Nazario," said Mourinho. "The only thing that came to my mind was a goal where I had the honour to be sat next to Sir Bobby Robson, in 1996, and Ronaldo Nazario scored a goal against Compostela from behind the halfway line and scored a very similar goal."

Asked if Son is a manager's dream given his humility and hard graft, Mourinho continued: "From the outside I had that feeling. I had a feeling, and the experience, not my experience but of some colleagues; I even remember speaking with Sir Alex about Ji-sung Park. It's probably a cultural thing, that players from that part of the world are very coachable, they like to learn and are very humble. I met his parents yesterday, and I understood also where it comes from. The kid is fantastic and I am so happy." Mourinho could be heard shouting to give Son the man of the match award when he was being interviewed by Sky Sports.

Harry Kane struck two hugely-impressive goals with shots from distance and Mourinho praised the skipper's all-round performance, but admitted he was already struggling for accurate accolades. "It's not just the goals, it's the combination play, it's what he does between the lines, it's what he does in the defensive process and it's what he does at a leadership level. Incredible. Again: top, top, top player and person. I cannot find any more words to describe him. I cannot have a bad feeling with these guys. I'm here to help them. So if I can help them to be better then that's what I want."

"[It was] a perfect day," the manager admitted, "No injuries, a clean sheet, goals, perfect football, kids coming on for first Premier League football. [Burnley manager] Sean Dyche is always honest and told me after the game we were too good for them. I thank him for that. They are difficult to play against but we were too good. It wasn't them that were bad. Finally the boys get a day off tomorrow that I've not been able to give them yet. Son's is a tremendous goal. Harry's two outside the box and the pass for the Moussa goal. A couple of better passes or choices we could have had more."

Troy Parrott made his Premier League debut as Mourinho spoke highly of the hardly-seen Parrott for what he did during the week. On why he gave the match ball to Parrott: "It was his debut and I think it had a much bigger meaning to a kid who last week was playing against kids in the Champions League. Today, he's playing in the Premier League at 17 - he's played for Tottenham in the Premier League, played for his country in a match in Dublin. I think it's an amazing week for him."

3: MAURICIO POCHETTINO

MAY 2014 to NOVEMBER 2019

MAURICIO POCHETTINO'S FINAL GOODBYE to his Spurs squad was a hastily scribbled message on a club tactics board. With no time to say his farewells face-to-face, Pochettino wrote: "Big thanks to you all! We can't to (sic) say goodbye.... you will always be in our hearts", with his signature at the bottom. The image of Poch's final farewell was tweeted by his assistant Jesus Perez.

It was a poignant end to a reign that had begun with the club in something of a crisis. Pochettino was named Tottenham boss on 28 May, 2014 after taking Southampton to their best-ever finish in the Premier League. Daniel Levy made an inspired appointment after he sacked Tim Sherwood. When Pochettino took over the club had managed only two top-four finishes in 22 Premier League seasons. After a fifth-placed finish in his first season at the club, he led them to third in 2015-16 - their highest final position in the Premier League. Pochettino guided Spurs to a number of top-four finishes, including runners-up to champions Leicester City in 2016.

Yet in a little over five years the Argentinian transformed the North London club. They became regular visitors to the knock-out stages of the Champions League and he masterminded the end of St Totteringham's Day as Spurs finally finished above Arsenal in 2017 after 22 years of ending the season lower in the table than their rivals. However it isn't just the improvement in Spurs' standing in the league that will leave an impression but the high-pressing, all action style of Pochettino's teams that had Tottenham fans recalling the 'Glory, Glory' days of the sixties and eighties when the club had a reputation as one of the most entertaining teams in the land.

In the end Pochettino's record in the north London derby wasn't amazing, in all competitions, he won four of 13 matches against the Gunners (won four, drew six, lost three), with only one of those victories coming away from home - a 2-0 win in the League Cup quarter-final last season. Nevertheless he took Tottenham from a mid table team into Top 4 regulars; after finishing fifth in his debut season the club qualified for the Champions League in each of the next four seasons finishing third, runner-up, third and fourth. However, he departed with Spurs 14th in the table with just three wins from 12 games in the Premier League.

Pochettino became the first opposition manager to beat Pep Guardiola in England when Tottenham defeated Manchester City 2-0 in October 2016 and Spurs continued to progress, finishing second and third respectively in the next two seasons. He led Tottenham to the last 16 of the Champions League in 2017-18 and was rewarded with a five-year contract in May 2018, yet trophies eluded him throughout his Spurs career. He lost an FA Cup semi-final to Mourinho's Manchester United in April 2018, Tottenham's eighth successive defeat at that stage of the competition and of course led Spurs to the Champions League final for the first time in their history the following season after a memorable and inspiring comeback against Ajax.

For five seasons the progress of Tottenham seemed clear and indisputable, yet the 7-2 crushing by Bayern Munich in the group stage of this season's Champions League seemed to signal the beginning of the end. He departed Spurs on 19 November 2019 having won just three Premier League games all season. His tally of 382 Premier League points ranked behind only Manchester City (446), Liverpool (404) and Chelsea (398) over the course of his reign.

Poch may have paid the price for a poor start to this season, sacked with Spurs 14th in the Premier League. Yet, he will be recognised as one of the great Tottenham managers for guiding Spurs to the Champions League final which assured the Argentine of his place in the club's history. He became only the third man to lead the club out in a major European final, while a consistent record over five years entitles him to be recognised as one of the clubs' finest managers.

He took charge of 293 games in all competitions, fourth in the club's all-time list. Only Bill Nicholson (832), Peter McWilliam (505), and Keith Burkinshaw (431) have been in charge longer and only the legendary Nicholson (55) led them in more European games than Pochettino (53).

The 47-year-old took charge of more Premier League matches than any other Spurs boss (202) and, before this season, he boasted the best points-per-game ratio of any Tottenham boss in Premier League history. However, after a poor start, (1.89) he dropped to second behind his predecessor Tim Sherwood (1.91), although Sherwood managed only around a tenth of the games.

His rank among Premier League managers, though, puts his record into firm perspective. For all the improvements at Tottenham, including the development of young players like Harry Kane and Dele Alli, he failed to win a trophy; and is still yet to win any trophy as a manager including spells at Españyol and Southampton.

Yet statistics favour Pochettino as he reached 100 Premier League wins as Spurs manager in just 169 games - only Mourinho with Chelsea (142) and Sir Alex Ferguson with Manchester United (162) got to that landmark for a single team in fewer games. Yet it was in the big matches that Spurs often fell short. Only Arsenal (51) picked up fewer points against fellow "big-six" teams than Tottenham (60) in his reign. Since August 2014, Spurs lost more Premier League games against those sides than any of those other teams (23). The table shows the results in matches between sides in the 'big six' in the Premier League since August 2014.

When Pochettino suggested before the Champions League final that winning that trophy might prompt him to leave the club, it seemed to many that the beginning of the end was closer than anyone expected. Arguably, perhaps he might wish he had left whatever the result of the Final!

During this calendar year 2019 Spurs have shown relegation form. No Premier League side has lost more matches in all

Pochettino's final message to his Spurs players

competitions than Pochettino's (18). Spurs last lost more games in a calendar year in 2008, when they suffered 19 defeats during spells under Juande Ramos and Harry Redknapp. A dismal away record has been the main issue, their last away league win came in January when they scraped an injury-time victory against a Fulham side destined for relegation. They also lost more points from winning positions than any other Premier League side (12), bringing into question the players' motivation.

Tottenham's tally of 14 points was their lowest after 12 games of a Premier League season in 11 years, and for a club in such a swish new stadium with so many England and international stars, this was a huge let down. Little wonder chairman Daniel Levy said results had been "extremely disappointing" and the manager paid the price, but there had also been simmering tensions behind the scenes.

The media were full of conspiracy theories. For example that back in July, as players returned for pre-season training, Pochettino wanted to install fixed cameras on the training pitches to record sessions, only for Levy to refuse to pay the £80,000 cost. The manager offered to pay, only for Levy to refuse permission to buy them.

Levy accepted £10m from Amazon to record a fly-on-the-wall documentary series documenting the club's season. As part of the agreement, fixed cameras were installed in Pochettino's office, they were not dissimilar to those he had requested to film training sessions! Managers generally consider their office to be a personal sanctuary.

The manager was the head of the playing department, and all requests related to first team matters to Levy go through the club's head of football operations, Rebecca Caplehorn, who sits above five heads of department, of which Pochettino was just one. Her remit is to run the club on a daily basis and communicate messages between department heads and Levy. A key part of her role is also to deal with recruitment and contract renewals for players and staff alongside the Spurs chairman.

After the Champions League final, Pochettino wanted to sell players he knew had no intention of staying at the club and could walk away for nothing at the end of the season: Eriksen, Vertonghen and Alderweireld. He wanted to raise funds to reinvest in a rebuilding the squad. But Levy and Caplehorn decided all three were to remain at the club, even if it meant losing them for free.

The negativity caused by such big influences within the dressing having such a big desire to leave had a toxic effect on the managers reliance on squad unity. There were supposed to be clear-the-air talks with Levy in August but the season started calamitously with a 3-0 defeat at Brighton following a 7-2 humiliation at home to Bayern Munich at the start of October. Spurs had won just twice in the Champions League against Red Star Belgrade as it seemed the club were preparing for his departure with the final route to an exit being the substantial compensation.

The 1-1 home draw against Sheffield United before the international break proved to be the manager's final game and Levy initially enquired about Leicester boss Brendan Rodgers but was told prising him away from the King Power Stadium would be impossible.

Spurs then turned to Julian Nagelsmann, but were told RB Leipzig's impressive rising young manager would be too hard to land having only just moved clubs in the summer and with no Premier League experience it would be asking a lot for him to hit the ground running at a time of a mini crisis with some fans fearing relegation. So perhaps that it was inevitable that preliminary soundings to the unemployed Mourinho were going to be finalised very quickly. Eddie Howe was also considered as the best young English manager option but had not as yet handled the big names stars at a big club so was again too much of a risk.

Mourinho had been holding out for the Spurs job as he rejected a number of alternative approaches and he bided his time working as a Sky sports pundit. The media had predicted that Pochettino would go into the clash with West Ham under even greater pressure than the under-fire Hammers boss Manuel Pellegrini but time was on Levy's side to sort out compensation issues and install Mourinho during the international break.

Pochettino's son Sebastiano quit Spurs' Sports Science team following his father's departure but his younger brother Mauricio has stayed on as a winger for the Under-23s. After achieving a First Class degree in Applied Sports Science from Southampton Solent University, Sebastiano was named Tottenham's Sports Science Assistant. He then headed the department from June 2017 until his exit. Highly-rated Mauricio, 18, was the only Pochettino left at Spurs. After signing his first pro contract in the summer he was one of the stars of the u-23s.

One of the shadows hanging over Poch's reign was the move to the new stadium. The last few days at White Hart Lane were memorable and emotional for those of who had first visited the old ground in our childhood and were there to see it demolished. And, although the new ground looked fantastic, the cost of it was always likely to have an impact on Poch's transfer budget.

All those concerns were forgotten however for 'An Evening With Glenn Hoddle' held at White Hart Lane in the last few weeks before demolition.

It was the Thursday night at the Lane, days before what would be the final game at the "world famous home of the Spurs" for the past 118 years. The invitation was marked "not to be missed" in my diary, immediately after it arrived from none other than arguably the greatest ever Spurs legend, Glenn Hoddle' as voted for by the experts. The final game was against Manchester United on 14th May 2017, but the invitation to the Lane was Thursday April 27 for "An Evening With Glenn Hoddle," one of the final club official functions inside the old Lane before it was due for demolition the morning after the United game.

Glenn picked me up at my home in Sunningdale as he lives not too far away, or rather his regular driver did; the one who normally ferries him to and from from the ITV studio on the South Bank, Waterloo, or to the BT Sport studios in Stratford.

The labyrinth of building works failed to distort the memories; scaling the old stone stairs as a kid to make my way to my season ticket seat in the old main stand, to the new stand development where I was a regular 'insider' either interviewing Glenn for his autobiography, or even invited into the inner sanctum, the board room, as guest of a number of owners. I even played on the pitch for a press team I helped to organise. Now, that was something! It was Gary Stevens comeback game after many months out injured and manager Peter Shreeves came into our dressing room to ask the media men to go easy on him. It worked okay for about 10 minutes. It didn't take Rob 'Shep' Shepherd long before he was steaming into a tackle on Gary! His column was very much like his tackle - over the top!

However, it was also an embarrassing end to my cameo role as a footballer. Trying to score with an elaborate near post diving header from a Trevor Brooking cross from the right, not only did I miss the ball completely, but the effort in stretching to try to do so, ended with me landing face down on the penalty spot with cramp in both legs and unable to move until helped from the field.

Irving Scholar also fancied himself as a footballer. Like myself, Irving was a Spurs nut, and leapt at the chance of run out on the pitch. His first attempt was also his last as he snapped his Achilles, ouch! Hence his arrival for the UEFA Cup Final, on the eve of him taking over as chairman, on crutches.

Back to the present, which would soon be back to the future. It was hard not to become engrossed in nostalgia as the huge cranes towered over the skyline adjacent to a building I was to enter for the last time as Glenn's guest. Up to the Board Room for the VIP meet and greet. Old friends Ossie Ardiles and Ricky Villa were there as they were stars of the show later that evening.

The main event was sponsored by Glyn Hopkin and Reynolds, and 'The Evening with Glenn Hoddle' was a huge success with an unmissable Q&A; an evening, 'Down Memory Lane' for me as well as Glenn, Ricky and Ossie.

Former players and staff were paraded on the pitch following the full-time whistle of the final Premier League match. Spurs wore a unique commemorative shirt, a special White Hart Lane crest with the words: "Tottenham Hotspur vs Manchester United, 14th May 2017". In addition to the new home kit, the team warmed up in a special edition training top, with the names of both sponsor AIA and the Tottenham Tribute Trust. All proceeds from the sale of the kit went towards the Trust.

The club posted regular updates, pictures and videos to keep their fans up to date with the progress of the build, with periodical media stories about the escalating costs. The club even had to make an official statement when one article suggested costs had leapt to an astonishing £1billion, the club announcing that costs were £750m, which were actually about twice as much as when the move was originally mooted.

There was also a touching announcement as the club said it would re-bury the ashes of Bill Nicholson at the new stadium. The remains of Nicholson, who died aged 85 in 2004, and those of his wife Grace were buried under the pitch until the stadium was demolished. The club moved the ashes to a spot where the White

Hart Lane pitch and the turf of the new stadium will overlap. Dear old Bill led Spurs to the 'Double' in 1960-61 and claimed eight major trophies in 16 years as manager following 17 years as a player. A private ceremony, attended by Bill and Grace's immediate family, was held to re-intern the ashes. Nicholson's daughter, Jean, said the move was a 'return home' for her father, whose remains had previously been held at a point overlooking the site while demolition work was completed. "My sister Linda and I are so grateful for the respect and affection that everyone at the club continues to show towards our father", Jean said. "There is no more fitting memorial than for him to rest below the new pitch, and having mum by his side makes it even more special. Dad's dream was always for his beloved Spurs to be the best in the world and it is clear that this new stadium project is a giant step towards that aspiration. We are proud that dad played a major role in developing the club's history and that his contribution is being remembered in this way. We're sure dad would have enjoyed watching the current team play, in the way that he always advocated. The fact that the Spurs are taking him with them into the future means so much to us all."

The new stadium has gone to host both football and NFL matches. Spurs must reassure their fans that it is football first, and only investment in the team will prove that to be the case. NFL UK managing director Alistair Kirkwood recalled how Levy was the mastermind behind this ambitious project. Kirkwood commented: "All the credit needs to go to Levy. We had various initial conversations with Spurs after they made the commitment to build the new stadium so the timing was good. Then you need someone like Daniel with the vision to do something that hasn't been done before and to think really big. It's a combination between the timing and the vision." NFL executives were taken aback initially when Levy came up with the suggestion that the new stadium could host American Football. The 62,000-capacity stadium is the first to include a dividing function, the innovative design will see the stadium be able to be transformed in 25 minutes, with the help of three 3,000-tonne steel trays.

Equally escalating values appeared almost monthly and with every new record broken by Harry Kane, about the goal-scorers transfer value, eventually suggesting he would fetch £300million! Far-fetched? Perhaps. However, Harry could become Britain's first £200m footballer if ever he was sold; and that would be tempting as it would cover a big chunk of the stadium costs. Then again, what's the point of trying to fill a 60,000 plus stadium without a team to go with it? And there were managers such as Pep Guardiola who felt that Spurs were the 'Harry Kane Team'.

Harry, though, continues to show no sign of itchy feet. He seems to be pretty straight forward. Another Alan Shearer. Almost dull in his single mindedness. Shearer chose Newcastle United, his home town, instead of Manchester United where he would have won a sack full of medals and trophies. Harry remains 'one of our own' and Pochettino said he would like him to become another Francesco Totti – a one-club man whose head would not be turned by the biggest clubs in the world. Totti was a rarity in the modern era at Roma, but Spurs are hopeful the same might apply to Kane – but much depends on the success of the team in terms of trophies. So the wait cannot go on much longer. If indeed more than another year.

Kane is a leader in the dressing room, every bit as influential inside the Spurs camp as John Terry was at Chelsea, or Stephen Gerrard at Liverpool. Spurs are not a one-man team, but not far short. Kane has become more important than Gareth Bale to the team. The highlight of the 2017-18 season was of course Tottenham securing qualification for the Champions League knockout phase with an outstanding display to beat holders Real Madrid on a memorable night at Wembley.

With Kane fit again after a hamstring injury, Spurs showed intensity and quality to make their mark on the Champions League after going out at the group stage the previous season. Dele Alli gave Spurs the lead after 27 minutes when he turned in Kieran Trippier's cross from close range, then doubled the advantage early in the second half with a shot that took a deflection off Real Madrid captain Sergio Ramos. Eriksen provided a cool finish from Kane's pass for the third and even though Cristiano Ronaldo pulled one back for Real with 10 minutes left, it was too little, too late, as Spurs made a powerful statement about their European aspirations. The only blip was the injury to Toby Alderweireld who came off with a hamstring injury in the 24th minute, and the Belgian took a long time to recover.

While Christian Eriksen had an exceptional season, and even in defeat against Juve there was some sparkling football at times, Kane paid the price for a late season ankle injury, as the season fizzled out with ahugely disappointing FA Cup semi-final defeat against Manchester United on their new adopted 'home' ground. But Spurs finished third and Kane remained the big hope for the club, almost as much as the ground move.

Glenn Hoddle went to the training camp to meet Kane and beat him in a ball-into-basket challenge! He knows Kane better than most. Harry is a perfectionist; he hired his own personal nutritionist when he felt he was carrying a touch too much body fat even though he didn't appear to be, and the result was that he speeded up and become even stronger, scoring more goals. When he first broke into the team, and started to score he was dubbed a 'one season wonder', and the fans remind everyone with a song to that effect!

Levy doesn't want to sell him at any price. Not even at £300m, despite Real Madrid and Manchester United making no secret of their desire to sign him. United have been on his trail for two years, and their then manager Jose Mourinho said he would join the bidding at £200m if there was ever a chance Spurs would sell. Now of course Jose is Spurs boss so there is almost no way the Portuguese would let him go.

Kane started out in the same junior club as David Beckham, but was rejected by Arsenal because he wasn't big or quick enough. Kane had his first Premier League start in 2014, winning the Golden Boot after scoring twenty-five goals in the 2015/16 season. He is the only likely candidate to beat Wayne Rooney's goals record for England.

Kane set a new record for the most Premier League goals in a year, finishing as Europe's leading scorer for 2017 after he bagged a brace against Southampton. Kane's 22nd-minute header at Wembley was his 37th goal of the year, moving him past Shearer's previous Premier League record, for Blackburn Rovers in 1995. Kane scored again with a close-range finish in the 39th minute. His second goal took him to 55 for club and country in 2017 – lifting him above Lionel Messi to become Europe's top-scorer over that 12 months in the five major leagues (England, Spain, Italy, Germany and France). Messi, who had 54 goals in the year, couldn't catch Kane as Barcelona didn't play again until 2018.

Kane was naturally 'proud' to have beaten two of the world's best players to the 2017 goal-scoring crown, but he made enormous personal sacrifices to get there. "They've been such good players over the last ten years or so, and dominated football and rightly so," Kane told ESPN of Messi and Ronaldo. "They'll go down as two of the best ever players. To even be up there and beat them is something I'm proud of. For me, it's about doing it every year. Not just beating them but winning as many trophies as they've won. I've sacrificed most of my time, especially with the schedule of games. You come in, you train, you play, you recover, you rest. That's a footballer's life. I don't complain. It's something I love doing. But you lose maybe the social part of your life. It's a matter of opinion. Not every player does what I do. Some players may go out, go for meals – that kind of thing. From my point of view, to get the best out of myself, it's about going home, resting, recovering, spending time with my family and do everything I can in that short period of time to achieve what I can."

I'm not knocking all the back-slapping, jubilation, and new records etc. But goals in a calendar year! Sorry to be a bit of a traditionalist (which I'm not really) but this is an ingenious new stat dreamed up by, well, those who love stats. It's goal per season, not per calendar year, surely?

Writing his Mail on Sunday column, Glenn Hoddle observed, "Harry Kane had a phenomenal 2017 and as a Spurs man I couldn't have been more delighted. The way I would sum up the impact he has as a striker is by saying: 'If Harry…' 'If Harry chases the ball down the like that …' 'If Harry lives his life off the field like that….' 'If Harry stays after training like that….' Sometimes you can have a star player who is a bit of a prima donna. The defenders can end up saying: 'Well, if he tracked back and worked properly, we wouldn't have so much to deal with.' But no one's got that excuse with Harry. He is a coach's dream. If he works as hard as he does to win the ball back, as the best player in the team, then there's no excuse for anyone else. He scores but he also creates and often he's making chances by harrying defenders into mistakes, which his team-mates benefit from. He's an inspiration for kids, having come through those tough loan-moves and got into the team. He's fought for everything he's achieved. He has everything: left foot, right foot, good head for goal, work-rate, enough speed and an understanding of when to move.

"If you built a robot, you would have all those attributes in there. And if a centre-half is worth now £75million, how much is he worth? It would have to be somewhere approaching Neymar's fee of £200m. There's only one fear I have. He had a really good season in 2015-16 but had run out of gas by Euro 2016. Even in the pre-tournament friendlies against Portugal and Turkey you could see he didn't have a run in him. And no player, not even Lionel Messi, can play like that. If Tottenham had a bigger squad they could leave Harry out for the odd game like Pep Guardiola does for Gabriel Jesus, Sergio Aguero, Raheem Sterling and Leroy Sane. But that option isn't there at Spurs. And it exposes a bigger problem coming down the line for the club. It may be that they can offer him the kind of money that would do justice to a player who has outscored Messi in 2017. But even if they can do that, can they put the players around him to make him feel he can win trophies? I said in the summer that this was a time for Tottenham to expand the squad with world-class players. I still feel that, though with the stadium needing to be financed it might have come a few years early to put themselves in the best position to keep Harry.

"I also believe that silverware breeds more silverware. So an FA Cup win can lay the foundations for a winning team. Winning the FA Cup in 1981 with Tottenham set our team up for a few years of success, going on to win the FA Cup again in 1982 and the Uefa Cup in 1984 and reaching the Uefa Cup quarter-finals, only losing to Real Madrid, in 1985. It was the launch-pad for our title challenge in 1984–85. I've nothing but admiration for the job Mauricio Pochettino is doing at Tottenham but he has spoken about how the Premier League and the Champions League are the trophies the club should target. And while he is right in the long term, in the short term the FA Cup might be a stepping stone. Spurs need trophies to persuade the likes of Harry Kane and Dele Alli to stay and be part of the next few years. The euphoria of an FA Cup win can help do that by creating lifetime memories. After all, it's almost 37 years since Ricky Villa scored for us at Wembley. And we're still talking about it!"

4: DAVID PLEAT

MAY 1986 to OCTOBER 1987

ASKED TO LIST TOTTENHAM'S GREATEST ever teams, David Pleat lists them in this order: 1. Bill Nicholson's Double winning team of 1960-61. 2 Mauricio Pochettino's team of 2016-17. 3. My Team of 1986-87. That is the considered view of one of football's deepest thinkers dating back to the 'Glory, Glory' years under captain Danny Blanchflower with Dave Mackay and John White.

Pleat is still involved at Tottenham as a consultant, and played a role in bringing Dele Alli to the club, and how back in 1987 Spurs should have beaten Everton to win the title. In fact so good were Spurs under Pleat they were in contention for three trophies but, much to Pleat's bitter disappointment, ended up with none. Always a man with powerful views about the game, his inside track on Daniel Levy is an eye opener for sure, while his opinion of Jose Mourinho is typically obtuse but first, to the side that still gives him so much pleasure, the 1986-87 team where Clive Allen scored a record 49 goals and in which Glenn Hoddle and Ossie Ardiles excelled.

"It was a wonderful year. I recall we beat West Ham 5-0 and played them again a few days later and beat them again. I got a wonderful letter from John Lyall their manager, a real gentleman. He wrote to me saying that I must be enormously proud of a side playing such wonderful football and doing so well. We went to Liverpool where the club hadn't won in something like 50 years and beat them. Clive Allen got a hat-trick in our first game, and I adopted a 4-5-1 formation with Clive up front long before managers such as Terry Venables were credited with such a tactical revolution.

"The truth is that pundits on TV are useless, they have no real idea of tactics. I've managed 1,000 games. We had a new system, and it worked so well that there was no one better than us that year. I just wish I had adopted it earlier as I am convinced we would have won the league that season instead of Everton. But it was a sad end to such a wonderful season of so much enterprise and promise. It was a big disappointment to have lost to Arsenal in our third game of the League Cup semi-final and then to Coventry at Wembley in the FA Cup Final, but as a football manager you have to live with the ups and downs.

"Whenever I see Spurs supporters, they always say to me that they remember the team of '87. In my view it was not quite as good as Poch's best team, but it was better than Venables team of '91 with Gazza and Lineker, but of course the best of them all was Bill Nicholson's Double winning team. What I loved about my team of '87 was that it wasn't an egotistical group, and it played football as good as anyone I'd seen over the years.

"Many people have plenty of opinions about me over the years, but of the first 50 games I was the most successful in the club's history, better than the so-called popular managers like Venables, Francis and Jol. That best winning percentage was because we were winning, winning, winning with that new formation."

Pleat has been Director of Football at Spurs and more recently "consultant", and is proud to have brought players like Dele Alli to the club. "I am very proud of that, very proud indeed, in fact very proud to have brought two or three of the most influential players in recent times to the club over the last eight years or so. So much has been said about Pochettino being the one who saw him play for MK Dons against Manchester United, but long before that I was watching him closely. I had six reports on him over a long period of time. I was told that it wasn't worth £5m to spend on a player from MK Dons that he wouldn't be good enough for Spurs, but that wasn't my opinion at the time."

Pleat respects how well Pochettino transformed the Spurs team, and is keeping his views on Mourinho to himself. When asked what he thinks of the new manager, he says "I am not going to tell you!" But he added significantly: "I want Tottenham to do well, and that means it doesn't matter to me who is in charge of the team, I genuinely want Tottenham to do well. They are in my blood, I love the club, always have and always will."

Pleat is reluctant to discuss Daniel Levy. Like the chairman, David Pleat is Jewish. Pleat is cautious when discussing the current Spurs chairman, but he said: "I get on fine with Daniel. I get on fine with everybody. But it amazes me the way some journalists and pundits go on about the Spurs chairman as if they know him. They don't. They have absolutely no idea what he is like. He is portrayed as hard-nosed. Don't you think every chairman is hard-nosed, tough, doing the best for their club, trying to get the best deal.

"The club has the best training ground, the best stadium. When Daniel first came into football at Spurs he had no football experience, he worked for Warner Brothers, but I coached him about the intricacies of the game and he has presided over a wonderful club, keeping salaries sensible and refusing to get caught up in football's mayhem. Yet Daniel Levy gets a bad press! Really? You have to ask yourself why that is. I could tell you why, but I am not going to."

Pleat was the Mourinho of his day in terms of touchline celebrations! He is best remembered by his famous 'dad dancing' celebration when he danced across the Maine Road pitch after Luton had avoided relegation on the last day of the 1982-83 season. Raddy Antic's late winning goal consigned City to the drop instead in one of the most dramatic moments of any top flight final day of the season.

I knew him back then when he was at Luton, but became much closer once he joined Spurs, and have kept in touch with him regularly over the years. David was once late for an hour long 5Live radio show I was appearing on, and listened to the beginning of the debate on his car radio. He eventually arrived half way through, and was intrigued to know how I knew, for sure, that Harry Redknapp would, indeed, be appointed the new Southampton manager. David had been acting as a consultant with

Portsmouth, so I would imagine he had a fair idea himself about what was going on behind the scenes. The following exchange went something like this…

"Where do you get your information from?" David asked me on air.

"You, of all people, should know where I get it from, David", I replied.

David and I go back a long, long way. Perhaps too long! And if anyone knows where I get my information form it should be him. I broke the story in the *Mirror* in 1986 that he would be the new Spurs manger following Peter Shreeves departure. He knew I was very close with the then Spurs chairman Irving Scholar. In fact, he never asked me at the time, and he must have noticed the *Mirror*'s back page headline as it was huge, that I knew for sure he would be named Spurs manager, so I can only assume he had a fair idea. What's more I also knew he was getting the sack from Spurs, something that hurt him deeply because it was for non-footballing issues.

Looking back, he now thinks that it was a "diabolical" decision to have sacked him and he should have been stronger and contested it and refused to go. "Maybe as these things go on in this industry someone had already been talking to Terry Venables to replace me, and I was subjected to diabolical media coverage. I have my own views about that. Don't ask me to elaborate!"

For Pleat it was a quick turn around form the heights of football management at the end of the 1986-87 season where he was being touted as a strong candidate to become the next England coach to losing his job at Spurs that October. After spells at Leicester, Luton (again) and Sheffield Wednesday he returned to Spurs as Director of |

Football in 1998 where he took the reigns during three caretaker spells between managers. Meanwhile he reinvented himself as an expert tactical analyst on TV and radio, and starred for ITV during their coverage of the 2006 World Cup. He has continued to work behind the scenes on disciplinary committees and for the Premier League on projects, his football knowledge still remains much sought after despite being 74, and now recovering from a serious illness.

For some time he did the "Chalk Board" feature for the *Guardian* newspaper, and back in 2010 he celebrated 50 years in the game by naming a team of the best players he had worked with - here are the Spurs contingent he selected for his personal all-time team/

RAY CLEMENCE

By the time I arrived at Tottenham Hotspur in 1986, Ray had already accumulated his major medals and experiences, yet he retained safe hands, was an intelligent player and a very good talker. Those are important qualities for any goalkeeper, and he was a reassuring last line of defence. Our exciting, adventurous 4-5-1 formation took all the plaudits as an attacking approach, but our defensive record was exceptional as well, and Ray took much credit for that. His influence was extensive. Our chairman, Irving Scholar, had wanted to put a camera in the dressing room to record our FA Cup final experience against Coventry – what proved to be our saddest day – and the players didn't fancy that. Scholar then suggested that the players need not know, and that we could put it in the ceiling, but I said that would be grossly unfair and tantamount to spying. I consulted Ray, as chief spokesman from the players' pool, and he said there was no way should happen under any circumstances. What happens in the changing rooms should be sacrosanct. Sure enough, the plan was eventually ditched. The irony is that, had the cameras been in there, they might have noticed that half of the team went out on the pitch with Holsten across their shirts and half didn't.

RICHARD GOUGH

We signed Richard from authoritarian manager Jim McLean at Dundee United, but his stay at Tottenham proved all too short. I met him to discuss terms at the West Lodge Park hotel and, while we were talking Ken Bates called up urging him not to sign for Spurs until he had spoken to Chelsea. Thankfully, he had made up his mind to come to White Hart Lane. At first his positional play needed adjusting as he was prone to embark on forays forward using his great athleticism, but he proved to be some player. He was a fitness fanatic and a natural leader of men, boisterous in the dressing room and a fine motivator of his team-mates. The type of player you wanted in your team. His father, Charlie, had played for Charlton Athletic and Richard was born in Sweden and brought up in South Africa. He was injured for the Cup final against Coventry and needed an operation on his knee, only to fly off back to South Africa immediately after the game. By the time he returned to London, he had made his mind up that he needed to move back to Scotland, with Graeme Souness at Rangers, having become homesick. Spurs doubled their money, but lost a top, top player.

GARY MABBUTT

He may have made his name at centre-half, but I first saw Gary at Bristol Rovers playing as a left-back. I was managing Luton at the time and tried to bring him to Kenilworth Road, meeting Gary and his father, Ray, who was a financial consultant and an ex-player, to discuss a possible move. We could have had him for a few pence more but the deal fell through – we joke now that our memories of the reasons the discussions came to nothing conflict – and Spurs were the ultimate beneficiaries. He was magnificent despite the circulation problems he'd suffer due to his diabetes. He was a great jumper for 5ft 10in, and tackled properly, rarely going to ground. To have come through the problems caused by his diabetes, and the horrific facial injury suffered against Wimbledon, was a magnificent achievement. A side with him and Donaghy in its defence would not have been relegated. They were 9-out-of-10 players every week, and totally reliable.

GLENN HODDLE

When I first met Glenn during the 1986 World Cup finals he had been promised that he could leave Tottenham that summer, but I persuaded him to stay on for another year. That season was undoubtedly his best at the club. He had outstanding vision and could play off the front foot, with that uncanny ability to play a pass away first time without having to adjust his feet or take the pace off the ball to get it on to his good foot. He had magical feet to play a ball with back-spin. He was also single-minded and quiet in the dressing room. We altered the position we asked him to play slightly to overcome the downsides to his game – he was never keen at tracking back or defending when possession was lost, as both Ron Greenwood and Keith Burkinshaw had noted. The 4-5-1 system relieved him of those defensive responsibilities as he became the loose second striker with his magnificent passing ability creating goalscoring opportunities for his team-mates. He eventually left for France and Arsène Wenger at Monaco, even though Spurs had originally struck a deal to sell him to Gérard Houllier at Paris Saint-Germain. He's had an interesting career path since, but he always had ideas on the game and I was not surprised when he took up coaching.

CLIVE ALLEN

Clive had this wonderful intuition as to when to take the ball on the half-turn and strike for goal. We played him across the width of the box and asked him not to put in any excess running or stray into wide areas. He wasn't the bravest, wasn't the quickest, not the most industrious and far from the biggest in the air, but he had an uncanny goalscorer's knack. As a person, he was first-class: a gentleman who knew that practice makes perfect, and would always stay out on a Friday when training had finished and rattle in half-volleys, volleys and shots into an empty net. His fabulous 1986-87 season started with a hat-trick at Villa Park and continued in similar vein all the way through to a record 49 goals. Reappointed by myself at Spurs several seasons ago, he remains a fine ambassador for the game.

DAVID GINOLA

David is a wonderful personality and a charming man who would sit down and have a conversation about football when most of the players were long gone from the training ground. It should be noted, too, that he would undertake extra training and was never in a hurry to leave – the cynics remarked that it was because he was standing in front of the mirror combing his air for 30 minutes after other players had left, but that was not so. He loved the game. He was a great dribbling talent and is the only player I ever worked with who was able to cushion the ball on his chest while in mid-air. It was his charisma as much as his skill that made him stand out. I remember him telling me once, in the nicest possible way, that 80% of the replica shirts we sold at Spurs had his name on the back. I think I respectfully told him that Tottenham never got involved with image contracts. He was asked to take on defensive responsibilities under George Graham's stewardship, but David was never that way inclined. A class act.

5: ARTHUR ROWE

MAY 1949 to APRIL 1955

A LOCAL TOTTENHAM LAD, ARTHUR FULFILLED his ambition to manage Tottenham, which he did with enormous success from 1949-1955, making his mark on the history of the game, let alone his beloved Spurs. If anyone thinks that the pressure of football management in the modern game with all its enormous rewards, is a pressurised business, it is sobering to think that one of management's greatest achievers suffered a nervous breakdown because of the pressure of trying to keep Spurs on top.

He made his managerial comeback with Crystal Palace and went on to spells at West Bromwich Albion, Leyton Orient and Millwall, but his golden years at White Hart Lane has its place in the club's rich history as the architect of Spurs' successful 'push-and-run' side.

Rowe had one of the sharpest football brains the English game has ever known and guided the club to their first ever League championship, in 1950-51. He left school in 1921, the year a Jimmy Dimmock goal took the FA Cup to White Hart Lane, and he signed amateur forms for Spurs in 1924. Rowe captained Spurs to third place in the old First Division in 1933-34 and won an England cap against France but the following season Spurs were relegated and wouldn't return to top flight football for 15 years. Injury curtailed Arthur's career in 1939 and he went to Budapest to spend two months as the official Hungarian government's instructor to their soccer coaches. He liked Hungary, a hotbed of football invention during the thirties, and was preparing to stay longer until war intervened and he returned to join the Army. Upon his demob in 1945 he took charge of Southern League Chelmsford, and in May

1949 he joined Spurs as manager: his salary £1,500 a year.

For three post-war seasons Spurs had average crowds of 50,000 plus on the terraces in the Second Division. Upon his arrival Rowe transformed the club with a team which included only a solitary newcomer, full-back Alf Ramsey. 'Push-and-run', they called it. "In fact, mate, it's just a case of doing the obvious. Football's a simple game, it's the players who make it difficult," Arthur said at the time. Spurs started with a 4-1 victory at Brentford and romped away with the Second Division title in 1950, and won the First Division in the same memorable fashion a year later.

Even when poor health led to his resignation, Arthur still left Spurs a legacy of style and one of his last signings – Danny Blanchflower – was to lead the club to a historic double at the start of the Sixties. Arthur once said, "All you need to remember is that 50 per cent of the people in the game are bluffers. So a decent manager's halfway there when he starts out." It seems that Arthur's maxim still rings true today!

Bill Nicholson played in the push and run team, and no doubt picked up a few managerial tips from his boss. Nicholson said, "Now and again a coach comes up with an idea which is seen to be original and is successful. Such an idea was the 'push and run' style introduced by Arthur Rowe at Spurs when he took over from Joe Hume. The team was at that time in the Second Division and not quite good enough to get out it. A former Spurs player in the years 1929-39, he was an attacking centre-half who, like me, won a single England cap.

"Arthur had this vision about the game which was summed up by the catch phrase 'make it simple, make it quick'. You learn from most of the coaches you work with and I learned a lot from Arthur. I had similar slogans in my managerial days. I believe they are necessary. You have to keep reminding players what they should be doing, because few of them are capable of acting instinctively

"Arthur was on the short side for a centre-half but was strong and good in the air. He was born in Tottenham and had a feeling for the place. A passionate talker and thinker, he had the advantage of working abroad for a short time in Hungary. I do not think, however, that his experiences there greatly influenced his approach to football; the Hungarians learned from us, from Jimmy Hagan in particular, rather than the other way round.

"The basis of push and run was keeping possession of the ball by quick, short and accurate passes. It demanded great skill, particularly in movement off the ball, and fortunately Tottenham had the players on their staff at the time capable of playing it effectively. It also demanded maximum fitness because it was not possible to play that way unless all ten outfield players were 100 per cent fit.

"In the 1949-50 season, when Tottenham were promoted with 61 points, the club used only 13 players and it was said we were lucky as regards lack of injuries. That may be so, but I believe good players are injured far less than average or poor players. If they are playing in a good side, there is continuity and flow about the play and they are supported to the hilt by their colleagues. They are not left to struggle on their own; there is always someone to pass to.

"Tottenham stayed at the top using 'push and run' for little more than three seasons. In Arthur Rowe's second season, 1950-51, the team won the First Division championship with 60 points, and the following season were runners-up to Manchester United."

Bill Nicholson pointed out that the average attendance at Spurs back then under Arthur was 54,405, during a period when Tottenham could boast the highest attendances in the country. The great man went on to say that it was a figure that would never be beaten unless the club built a new ground – which of course they have done now!

When I came to writing Bill Nicholson's life story, and detailed his thoughts about some of the wonderful players he managed, he made it clear that his favourite player to date was from Arthur Rowe's push and run team, Ronnie Burgess. "Ron is the first player I would select in the 'best ever' Tottenham side. He had all the requirements of the perfect footballer. He was well-built at just under six foot in height, with tremendous stamina, speed and agility and had great control and mastery of the ball. He was also a magnificent tackler, a good header of the ball and a brilliant passer.

He could strike the ball equally well with either foot and was a sound positional player."

6: OSSIE ARDILES

MAY 1993 to OCTOBER 1994

"IN POCH WE TRUST" WAS A KEY SLOGAN OF SO many of Ossie Ardiles' Twitter posts as the World Cup winner was much respected by Mauricio Pochettino and part of his inner circle. Little wonder Ossie was distraught by his pal's sacking. The feeling was much more personal and intense as Ossie is also a highly respected Global Ambassador for the club and has a high profile on every match day at the glittering new stadium as indeed he was at the old lane.

The former Spurs superstar and one time manager thanked his compatriot for his achievements at the club in a series of tweets while abroad in Punta Cuna, looking as though he was spending much of his time playing his beloved golf while all the action was back in north London.

"Mauricio put us in the elite of world football," tweeted the 67-year-old FA Cup winner. "We owe him so many memories. Where to start? With him we learned to believe. Everybody at Spurs owes him so much. It was such a pleasure to arrive at the training ground and witness the camaraderie, the atmosphere. From my personal point of view, life gave me a wonderful present. Unique. His friendship. The friendship of a wonderful, principled man that would last forever."

Ossie Ardiles entered football management after an illustrious playing career where he won a World Cup winners' medal with Argentina in 1978, then signed for Tottenham Hotspur and became a fan favourite. A midfield dynamo renowned for his short passing, he was simply a delight to watch, and linked up brilliantly with Glenn Hoddle. He was signed by Keith Burkinshaw in the wake of Argentina's World Cup triumph and went on to twice win the

FA Cup before adding a UEFA Cup at White Hart Lane.

In July 1989, Ardiles was appointed manager of Swindon Town and he began to transform their style of play, leading the club to their highest-ever league finish but despite winning the second division play-offs in 1990, the club were denied a place in the First Division due to financial irregularities. The following season he was instructed to sell players because of the financial crisis and before long Ardiles was offered the job at Newcastle United, however his spell at St. James Park was a disaster with the club languishing at the foot of the Second Division table when he was sacked. Ardiles moved on to Third Division West Brom and guided them to promotion with a 3-0 victory over Port Vale at Wembley. Before long the inevitable happened and Ardiles was offered the manager's job at White Hart Lane in 1993 in what would prove to be a roller-coaster ride.

Under the enigmatic Alan Sugar Spurs splashed the cash on World Cup stars Jurgen Klinsmann, Illi Dumitrescu and Gheorghe Popescu but the team were far too inconsistent and finished 15th. Ossie's last game in charge came a few months into the following season in a 3–1 win over West Ham. A day later Alan Sugar sacked Ardiles, and appointed Gerry Francis in his place. Ossie's sacking came as no surprise as the exciting performances of the start of his reign had been replaced by too many defeats with little attention to defensive play and a Cup shock at Notts County where Spurs lost 3–0 to a side with only one win all season who were rooted to the bottom of Division 1.

In the words of Alan Sugar, from his autobiography, 'What You See Is What You Get', that night at Notts County was Ossie's undoing. It was that evening in the directors' lounge at Notts County that Sugar and the other directors present decided that he would have to go. On the Sunday after the win over West Ham Ardiles was summoned to Sugar's house where he was told that, sadly, he would have to leave.

In his autobiography, 'Ossie's Dream', Ardiles describes his thoughts. "The hardest thing that's happened to me in my life was leaving Tottenham. The blackest time, after the Malvinas aftermath, was my departure from Tottenham. My life changed completely after that. Tottenham is my home, my family, my everything. I sincerely believe, have always believed, that I was destined to manage Tottenham. There is a way of being that we share, a footballing identity that both I and the club have. I've always known that if I was asked to manage Barcelona, Real Madrid, any legendary club or Tottenham, I would choose Tottenham every time. Without hesitation. I was born to play for Tottenham and to manage Tottenham. So when I did get to manage Tottenham it was quite literally a dream come true."

Being sacked hit Ardiles hard but he knew it was coming. "The season had started well with those wins against Sheffield Wednesday and Everton, but as it progressed there were a few results that weren't exactly good for us and the whole five forwards issue was aired again. Perhaps I was too stubborn…"

Indeed, Ossie had been stubborn. In particular he was stubbornly loyal to his assistant Steve Perryman. With my personal relationship with Ossie, and also with the chairman, I did all I could to save Ossie from the axe. I suggested to Sugar that bringing in a defensive coach of the calibre of Don Howe might help. Don was up for it. Ossie 'Famous Five' were sensational going forward but defensively there were too many gaps, they were left wide open too often. Howe would close those gaps. Sugar went for the plan, Ossie thought about, but said that was Perryman's job and he would not go for it.

Ossie went on: "The key match, the one I got sacked after, was against Notts County in the Coca-Cola Cup. The night of 26 October 1994 was wet, dark and cold – horrible. When we arrived at Meadow Lane with Tottenham and all its stars I remember feeling that it was a recipe for disaster, We had already conceded two goals in the first half when Dumitrescu got sent off. We were down to ten men. We lost the tie 3–0. I think of it as my black night. I knew my time was up.'

As Tottenham beat West Ham the following Saturday at least Ardiles left on a high. He was called to the Chairman's house the next day. 'Alan Sugar fired me (although he never actually said

Ricky Villa, Ossie and I during a promotional lunch at Planet Hollywood in London's West End. The World Cup winners made a huge impact not just on Spurs but the whole of English football.

"You're fired"). I genuinely think he was sorry. He had to do it, in a sense. He felt a change was necessary. The fires had been quashed, the squad was superlative, and he thought another manager could pick the baton up and run with it."

Ossie thinks that in hindsight he should not have gone to Spurs when he did. It was a very difficult time at the club and he feels he would have been better to have waited for the opportunity to manage the club later in life. He admits that being sacked from Spurs was very hard for him and it has taken him a very long time to get over it. "I've never quite got over the hurt of how things turned out. I spent years not going back to the club at all. Not once, for many years. Now I do go to games and feel closer to the place again, but until very recently if you asked me when did I finally get over all the disappointment I would honestly have to say, 'Oh, any day now…' I am over it now, and really feel part of the

Tottenham family again."

Ardiles is a Tottenham legend and along with Ricky Villa is always given a warm welcome by supporters at White Hart Lane where Ossie is now a global Ambassador. Ossie will always be loved by Spurs fans.

Since managing Spurs, Ardiles has also had managerial spells in Croatia, Mexico, Japan, Israel, Argentina and Paraguay. He has won a number of awards in management which include winning the Nabisco Cup with Shimizu in 1996, the Tokai Cup with Shimizu S-Pulse in 1996 and 1998 as well as the Emperor's Cup in 2005 with Tokyo Verdy 1969. He was also named J. League Manager of the Year in 1998.

Ossie Ardiles and Ricky Villa have been friends of mine for many years, and it was a great pleasure for me to 'direct' a 60-minute film documentary on the life and times Ossie. The Legends Lives documentary Ossie was filmed with the World Cup at Wembley, in the Spurs dressing rooms beside the shirts of current heroes Kane and Alli, and striding out at the Lane for the very last time before the stadium redevelopment. A stellar cast were lined up to be interviewed to tell some enthralling inside stories about Ossie – Mauricio Pochettino, Jurgen Klinsmann, Chris Hughton, Teddy Sheringham, Glenn Hoddle, Garth Crooks, Ricky Villa, Mario Kempes, and Gerry Armstrong, among them.

For the film, I obtained an exclusive interview with Jurgen Klinsmann, who set up the filming personally out in LA, such is the German superstars admiration for Ossie that he was keen to take part in the film. Jurgen said in the film that he will always be grateful to Ossie for bringing him to English football. Klinsmann striker partner Teddy Sheringham told the story of how Ardiles wanted to sign Diego Maradona for Spurs but changed his mind and signed Klinsmann instead. But Klinsmann says, in a video clip he personally delivered for the Ossie Ardiles film, that his footballing career was inspired by watching Ardiles win the World

Ossie, Ricky and I at the filming of the Living Legend documentary. Ossie still lives in England over 40 years on.

Cup. "When I think of Ossie Ardiles, many, many things come into my mind. One major point was that I was 14 when I watched him playing in the 1978 World Cup, watched Argentina win the World Cup and his performances were admirable. His style of playing, his creativity, he was an inspiration, a master of the game.

"Many years later he became my coach and probably made the biggest change in my life when he brought me to Tottenham. I got the experience of English football through his eyes, his vision, his character and for that I will always be grateful. What I liked most about him was that he was always open minded, open to taking risks, never satisfied, as he always wanted to explore things and try things. Sure, it was a little bit risky – five forwards all the time! But it was fun!

"His personality was admirable, he reached out to people, he reached out to see the world. South America, Japan for many years, Paraguay, was one station, Israel another station, he never stopped. You had to admire that his brain was always seeking out new horizons, constantly challenging himself. For that he was a role model with what he has done, what he has achieved in his life – simply amazing."

Such was the close relationship between the two Argentines, Ardiles and Pochettino,

that Mauricio was more than willing to offer his personal tribute in my film. Talking in the film the then Spurs manager said, "He represents a legend, not only for Tottenham, but for world football, and for Argentina he is one of the most important players ever. It was very special for me especially as I was six years old and I listen and the names I hear were Ardiles, Passarella, Kempes, so for me he was one of the best in the world. He is forever in the history of world football and he will always be a legend in football."

Former Spurs manager Terry Neill also took part in the film and he revealed it was "the worst decision of my managerial career" that he didn't sign Ardiles and Villa for the Gunners! But Neill, an Arsenal man in his heart and soul, contacted then Spurs manager Keith Burkinshaw with the idea of signing Villa while he was signing Ardiles. Neill always denies this part of the story

It was a privilege to meet Ossie,
Diego and his then wife Claudia on a visit to London

whenever I let him know that I know. He insists that the Arsenal board vetoed any foreign signings as he had also lined up Johan Cruyff.

Ardiles still lives in England and speaking from his home in the Hertfordshire town of Hoddesdon, he told of his sheer joy of having been associated with Spurs for so long, "It has been a brilliant 40 years, an extraordinary adventure and, of course, I am still here. White Hart Lane has been a second home, not just for me, but for all the friends I've made in that time. My team-mates and the supporters as well.

"I must say when I first arrived the food was pretty terrible, we were not used to it at the beginning and we both had steak every day. But little by little over the years it has improved and now of course London is the food capital of the world. As for the weather, well, very bad, very bad. Now though I am used to it. It makes you appreciate it a lot more when the sun shines – there's always a silver lining, even to the weather here.

"I was very lucky to have arrived here with Ricky in '78, because England now is much more different to the England then, nothing like it is today. We were the first two, and at the time, no I didn't have a clue the impact it would make. Yes, I understand it now. Back then it was a great, great adventure, a big, big adventure, but it was good to be with Ricky."

Ricky Villa achieved Tottenham immortality for one of the best ever – if not the best ever – Wembley FA Cup Final goal. Yet it was Ossie's winning mentality that delivered important trophies to the Lane, but also arguably one of the most catchy Cup Final songs. "Ossie's Going To Wembley, His Knees Have Gone All Trembly. Come on You Spurs, Come On You Spurs", were the lyrics to the Chas & Dave song that has lingered longer than most Cup Final songs. It's still dusted off and sung with gusto by Spurs supporters, at the merest hint of an FA Cup run. Ossie admits he hated it at first but the song grew on him! "It's a beautiful song, from when we won the FA Cup in 1981," he said "In the final, when Ricky scored such a wonderful goal. Although it all happened in 1981, it is still very much in the hearts of every Tottenham supporter. I didn't like it when I first heard it, but because the supporters remember the song it has become a beautiful song – but I am very, very surprised that the supporters still like it. I am very pleased when they now sing this song."

When asked about Ossie's greatest moment in English football he has little hesitation, "Well it was winning the 1981 FA Cup Final. We had a wonderful team, full of flair and quality, but up until that point we had won nothing. Winning the FA Cup gave us the confidence to be an even better team. Yes, there has been a lot of ups and downs, but I wouldn't change a thing. And to prove how much I love the country, and Spurs, I am still here, of course."

Ricky Villa regularly comes to stay with Ossie, especially around Cup Final time, when he is much in demand. Ossie says: "When I first arrived I immediately felt that Tottenham was my second home and I always will. The more I stayed in this country, the more it felt like my second home."

Glenn Hoddle was voted by his fellow Spurs legends as the greatest ever legend of the north London club, but Ossie was in the running. For the man himself, however, there was only one winner,

"For me Glenn Hoddle was Spurs greatest player of all time. I have heard that Bill Nicholson would have selected Ronnie Burgess, and many fans would go for Dave Mackay, but it is so hard when I have seen neither of these players. However I played with Glenn and I have seen him in training and in games, and he is the best as far as I am concerned. He was a genius."

Ardiles felt most honoured when Miller suggested that he would come out on top.

Spurs centre-half Paul Miller played alongside Ossie and Glenn in that memorable eighties Spurs team, asked to name his favourite Tottenham players he said, "this club has had some real greats and it is hard to examine the credentials of players you haven't seen, but Mackay is right up there, so too is Pat Jennings, and of course Glenn Hoddle, but I would vote for Ossie or Dave Mackay."

7: HARRY REDKNAPP

OCTOBER 2008 to JUNE 2012

HARRY REDKNAPP LOOKS BACK AT HIS TIME as Spurs manager with a great deal of fondness and an enormous amount of pride as he makes a contribution to the book on Spurs managerial successes and failures. He nominates Bill Nicholson as the undisputed greatest ever manager, so Jose Mourinho has some way to go to topple Billy Nick. He said without hesitation that Nicholson would be No1 greatest every Spurs manager.

After that Harry knows that Keith Burkinshaw and Terry Venables enjoyed some degree of success with their trophies and style of football. "After Billy Nick, I wouldn't really know", he said, "Keith obviously won trophies, so too did Terry, but Spurs were still very much considered a mid table team." Here is where Redknapp takes such enormous pride in lifting Spurs into the Champions League for the first time in the club's history, which took them to another level.

As for the worst ever Spurs manager, "I wouldn't like to say", but while he didn't think managers such as Ramos or Santini achieved very much, he didn't think Tim Sherwood's short reign was that bad!

Over in Germany filming a second edition of 'Harry's Heroes', Redknapp looked back on his personal highlights as Spurs boss when he told me: "Winning at Manchester City to qualify for the Champions League gave me enormous satisfaction, and that competition certainly provided some magic moments, winning in Milan against such a formidable team at that time with so many incredible players, it was such a fantastic night. Beating Inter Milan, well we actually absolutely murdered them, and that was something,

A convivial lunch with Harry at Langan's Brasserie in Mayfair.
His Spurs reign paved the way for the club's current high status..

it was such a great performance.

"I had a great time, and I think we had a great team. It was enjoyable, I loved it, we played some great, exciting attacking football; two wingers every week, Lennon and Bale, Modric in midfield, such open attacking football, it was a joy to watch."

Tottenham took a step closer to the Champions League quarter-finals with a surprise 1-0 victory over AC Milan at the San Siro in February 2011. Redknapp's side were brimming with confidence going into the second leg after comprehensively seeing off the Serie A giants in a dramatic encounter. Spurs had already caused trouble for the Rossoneri's fierce local rivals Inter Milan in the group stages with a pulsating 4-3 loss to Inter back in November with a Bale hat-trick, then the 3-1 victory in the reverse fixture. Now Peter Crouch hit home a superb winner late in the second half, Lennon was the genius behind the goal, breaking away with an electrifying run and evading Milan defender Mario Yepes to feed Crouch in the box, who made no mistake rolling a perfectly-timed finish home 10 minutes from time.

Redknapp also had success in taking Spurs up the table to be a respectable challenger at the top end. "We didn't do too badly in the league, did we? Top four finishes, 5th place, all we really needed was one or two important signings to really push on, but all I got at a crucial time was a couple of loan players to fill in!"

While Harry sounds as if he might still have a chip on his shoulder about being sacked by Daniel Levy, that's far from the case.

Were there any lingering issues with the chairman? "No" came the blunt reply.

Was he harbouring any regrets? "No, none really, it doesn't bother me, these things happen. But I haven't been to the new stadium I've not been to the new training ground."

Have you not been invited? "No, but I've no problem with that. If I wanted to see the new ground I can buy my own tickets."

Well, he can certainly afford the tickets, having become a newly discovered TV celebrity! Reinvented as a leading TV pundit, winner of "I'm A Celebrity Get Me Out Of Here", and consequently much in demand from sponsors and coveted as a guest speaker, the one-time Spurs manager is the go to man for comments about Mauricio Pochettino's sacking and the appointment of Jose Mourinho. Before Mourinho's appointment Redknapp commented, "Someone will walk in there, a new face, a new voice to take over a team that is as low as they could go and he will lift them. It is a great time to come and manage Tottenham Hotspur. Whoever comes in, the only way is up because they cannot go any lower than where they are at the moment in the Premier League. There could not be a better time to take the job, it is a great time for someone to become Tottenham manager."

Redknapp believed Spurs should not appoint a big-name foreign manager and instead opt for and Englishman. Asked who he thought should be the next manager, he said: "Chris Wilder at Sheffield United. What the boy's done... that's amazing. But he won't get a look in, they will end up going for another big name who is not as clever as him. Wilder could win league titles with the right club in the Premier League. But English managers don't get a chance, they will go foreign again - they won't look at [Bournemouth manager] Eddie Howe."

Redknapp added: "Go through the squad, man for man in every position, it is full of internationals, every cover position is too. They have the best centre-forward in the world in Harry Kane, Son Heung-min, Dele Alli, it is an unbelievable squad but they have massively under achieved. This year they do not look like reaching the Champions League, which is not good enough for (owner) Joe Lewis and Daniel Levy, they must have Champions League football now with the stadium and training ground. They are hoping to bring someone in now who can do the magic and get them into the Champions League."

After Mourinho's appointment, which hardly fitted 'Arry's specifications, he said: "I love Mauricio Pochettino, but he has been averaging a point a game over the last 25 games. The Tottenham board are ruthless businessmen, they will have realised that at this rate they might not make the top four. Also the same voice after six years starts to wear a little thin, a new man can find another 10%, they will find a spring in their step for Jose's first game.

"The talk today has been about how the players loved Pochettino. Well if they loved him so much, why didn't they start playing better and winning some matches for him? They won't be losing any sleep. The ones who are in the team love you, the ones who aren't in the team hate you. Their wives hate you, their kids hate you. That's how football is."

Despite Mourinho's diplomatic response to what he might do to change the personnel in his team, Redknapp was sure the incoming manager already knew his January transfer targets. "Those who don't want to be there, he'll bomb them out in January, if you don't want to play," Redknapp said on The Debate. "He'll have three or four players lined up already. He knows all the right people, he'll have players lined up to come in. And those that can't make their mind up if they want to play for Tottenham he'll go 'No sorry, I only want players that want to be here, off you go'."

Harry Redknapp, Peter Crouch, Piers Morgan and Martin Keown were at the Hollywood Arms pub in Chelsea debating the firing of Pochettino and the hiring of Mourinho *Sportsmail's* inaugural A Pint with Piers. By coincidence, Redknapp's nephew, the Chelsea manager, was downstairs enjoying a pint at the bar with wife Christine!

Harry, you know what Tottenham chairman Daniel Levy is like. You've been hired by him. "And I've been fired! It was a shock when I got fired, believe me. I'd finished fourth in the Premier League, made the Champions League. Chelsea finished sixth but went and won the Champions League, so they got in, we dropped out, and that was the end of me."

You took over from Juande Ramos and, like Mourinho, you were announced as Tottenham manager the morning after your predecessor was sacked.

"I'd spoken to Daniel before they sacked the manager. Do you not think he's been talking to Mourinho all week, for the last two weeks? Of course he has. Daniel is not going to walk in yesterday morning and go, 'Right, we've sacked Poch, now let's have a look at that list'. Nah, it's all been done."

Redknapp dismissed Mourinho's' "I'll Never Manage Spurs" comment, as he made it clear that have coaching badge will travel! He explained: "Why would Pochettino say he'd never manage them? If Arsenal ring him tomorrow: 'We've got a five-year contract, £10million-a-year plus whatever', he'd be over there like a shot. Don't kid yourselves. In a week, he (Pochettino) will be forgotten! He'll be history. It'll be 'Mourinho, Mourinho, Mourinho'."

Martin Keown asked: "So do you think Tottenham did the right thing getting rid of Pochettino?

Redknapp: "No. Listen, you're dealing with Joe Lewis, who is the most ruthless businessman. They've got that stadium, the training ground. People keep saying they need another striker. So you want a striker. Peter comes in. 'Where do you see me playing boss?' I say, 'Well you won't play, you'll be on the bench, but when Harry (Kane) is not fit, you'll play'.

Joker Crouch said: "I'm up for that! Where do I sign?"

Redknapp: "You're always only six games from the sack. The owners of the club are worried they will not make the Champions League."

Crouch: "That's why they have been so ruthless".

Crouch though didn't think they would make the top four, as that looked destined for Leicester and Chelsea.

Turning to Piers Morgan, he made it clear that Arsenal as well as United would be thinking about whether they ought to go for Pochettino, and if so, when would be the right time to approach his advisors, presumably right away, even though they might not sack their current managers immediately. He said: "Let's be honest, Piers, do you think the Manchester United chairman has not woken up this morning and thought, 'Oh'. The chairman of West Ham has not woken up and thought, 'Oh blimey, Pochettino'. And the chairman at Arsenal.

Martin Keown agreed: "A few managers will be looking over their shoulders. Just 170-odd days ago, he's managing in the Champions League final. Now he's out of the job."

Redknapp: "They've been averaging a point a game for the last 25 (1.12 in the league to be exact). That's relegation form.

As Piers said: "Don't you think it is comical how Spurs fans are weeping for Pochettino but he won absolutely nothing in five years. Mourinho, they're moaning but he's won eight league titles in four different countries."

While Keown said Pochettino "won our respect", Morgan came back: "He won Arsenal fans' respect by winning no trophies!"

Keown added: "But now Arsenal fans might be looking at him with great interest, wanting him to go there.

"There are a lot of question marks about Mourinho, particularly with the way he finished at Manchester United. He'd lost the players, lost the dressing room, a few scathing comments. He was suffocating those players at Manchester United in his quest for greatness, because he is a serial winner. He has to be careful he does not do that in this Spurs dressing room. He has to nurture these players. None of these scathing comments in public. In a dressing room, if your manager keeps hammering you in the Press, you don't want that. There are two Mourinhos, and we don't know which one will turn up. The first one that seems to nurture, be your friend, mentor you. The second one is scathing. Mourinho is high risk. Which manager does he remind you of the past, Brian Clough? How many days did he last at Leeds? Forty-four?"

Does Mourinho get Tottenham into the top four?

HR: "I've just had a £100 bet with Piers."

PM: "No. It'll be Liverpool to win the league, Manchester City second, Chelsea third and Leicester fourth."

MK: "It depends which Jose turns up. If he is prepared to work with the players, put that ego - and it is one hell of an ego - to one side, nurture these players…"

Redknapp was sacked by Levy after almost four years in charge, with many believing it followed a fall out after being heavily linked with the England job and indicating that he would be interested in taking it before the FA went for the safer option in Roy Hodgson. The 65-year-old had a year left on his contract but failed to agree a new deal with Levy despite being in talks for some considerable time, although those talks dried up around the time he had been linked with taking over the England team.

Redknapp was hugely popular at the Lane despite initial misgivings by the fans. He brought back some of the most exciting times in recent history, but much like Pochettino, he didn't actually bring home a trophy.

"I have thoroughly enjoyed my time at Spurs and am proud of my achievements," Redknapp said at the time of his departure. "I have had a fantastic four years with the club, at times the football has been breathtaking. I am sad to be leaving but wish to thank the players, staff and fans for their terrific support during my time there." Levy thanked Redknapp in a statement on the club's official website: "This is not a decision the board and I have taken lightly. Harry arrived at the club at a time when his experience and approach was exactly what was needed. This decision in no way detracts from the excellent work Harry has done during his time with the Club and I should like to thank him for his achievements and contribution. Harry will always be welcome at the Lane."

The extent of Redknapp's success at White Hart Lane can be gauged by the circumstances of his arrival. Harry joined Spurs from Portsmouth in October 2008 with the club four points adrift at the bottom of the Premier League with only two points from eight games. Redknapp led Tottenham to eighth in the table with 51 points that season and a year later Spurs secured fourth spot and qualified for a first ever Champions League campaign in 2010. The following season the finished fourth again and only missed out on a repeat crack at the elite European tournament when Chelsea won the Champions League.

Redknapp was installed as favourite to replace Fabio Capello as England boss after his exploits with Spurs, and he has since admitted that he would have left Spurs had he been offered the job. When Capello left his post as England boss on 8 February, Spurs were third in the league, 10 points clear of a faltering Arsenal but they eventually finished a point behind the Gunners. Levy was disappointed by Spurs' end-of-season slump, and felt that the link with the England job had deflected his manager's attention from the job at hand, a charge Redknapp has always denied.

Redknapp consistently rejected suggestions that Tottenham were affected by the speculation linking him with England and publicly declared shortly before he was sacked that uncertainty over the stalling of his new contract could cause problems in the Tottenham dressing room. He said at the time: "The simple situation is I've got a year left on my contract. It's up to Tottenham whether they want to extend that contract or not. If they don't extend it and I go into my last year, it's not an easy one when players know you've only got a year left. It's up to Tottenham. If they think I'm OK and I've done a decent job and deserve an extension, they'll give it to me." However Levy thought otherwise. Having been the longest-serving Spurs manager since Terry Venables, whose reign ended in 1991, Harry was shown the door.

Spurs glorious run in the 2010-11 Champions League was eventually ended by Real Madrid in the quarter-finals. At the turn of the year they were considered potential title challengers but a run of one victory in nine matches saw them slip to fourth and lose out to Chelsea for the final Champions League place.

Andre Villas-Boas replaced Redknapp in the summer of 2012, signing a three-year contract with Levy prepared to give him a second chance and the benefit of the doubt after he was sacked by Chelsea. However, it was clearly a big error by the Spurs chairman as AVB was sacked just 17 months later following a chastening 5-0 defeat to Liverpool. "Daniel Levy is an expert in sacking managers. There's no time for long-term projects in the Premier League," AVB told ASPIRE4SPORT. "At Tottenham I learnt to be different. At Chelsea the group was more important, I stuck to my methods too much." Despite having the best win percentage, 55%, for Tottenham in the Premier League era and winning all six of his Europa League games, heavy defeats in big matches in his second season led to his three-year deal being cut short by the so-called "mutual consent" which invariably means "sacked".

8: MARTIN JOL

NOVEMBER 2004 to OCTOBER 2007

S PURS SPENT NEARLY A YEAR LOOKING FOR A successor to Glenn Hoddle. Following David Pleat's third spell in caretaker charge at the club, the board went for Lyon manager Jacques Santini but the Frenchman resigned after just 13 games in 2004 and his assistant Martin Jol stepped up to take the manager's seat which by then was a poisoned chalice. Despite a slow start, the fans quickly took to the likeable Dutchman and after a solid first season then recorded two back-to-back fifth place finishes – at the time Spurs' highest in the Premier League.

But after spending big in the summer of 2007, rumours began to circulate about Jol's position after an opening day defeat at Sunderland. With Tottenham flattering to deceive at the start of the 2007-08 season, Martin Jol looked set to lose his job after a heavy influx of arrivals including Gareth Bale. There was also a feeling among Spurs directors that a row earlier in the week before his sacking week between Jol and striker Dimitar Berbatov was a clear sign the manager had lost the backing of his players. There were also tensions with director of football Damien Comolli.

Jol managed just shy of 150 games, winning 45% of them, but results continued to be shaky. Despite strong backing from fans, pictures of Spurs directors meeting Seville boss Juande Ramos signalled the beginning of the end for Jol. The Dutchman finally learned of his fate in farcical fashion; at half-time during a group stage UEFA Cup match against Getafe! As rumours swirled around the White Hart Lane press box suggesting the Dutchman was about to be sacked, Spurs did the unthinkable and announced the decision that Ramos had taken charge in the middle of a match! It was little wonder the team went down 2-1 on the night and supporters left the game with the team managed by a different manager to the one who was in charge when they arrived at the ground, which is surely a unique occurrence in first class football! Later Spurs insisted that Jol had not in fact been sacked until after the Getafe game but Jol knew long before the final whistle that his time was up after receiving a text message from a friend during the match telling him he was to be fired.

I had the pleasure of writing Martin Jol's autobiography back in 2007, when he very kindly supplied the following first person Foreword for that book. He wanted the fans to "cherish my pride and satisfaction of having been part of the history of the great club that is Tottenham Hotspur." Martin's reflections on the day he was sacked mid-game make fascinating reading to this day.

I still don't really know the full truth about all that went on the day Spurs finally decided to sack me. But it is important that everyone realises that I did not know I had been sacked before the game, and that I was only told, officially, after it. Had I been told before the game, I would not have taken the team out, I would not have sat on the bench or been in the right frame of mind to lead out the team that night. I just couldn't have done it.

When the final whistle went, my nephew Robert ran over to me and told me to go left when we went down the tunnel into my own dressing room. He had heard on BBC radio that I had been sacked. He said to me: "They've sacked you". That was the first I knew about it. The club secretary John Alexander came into my dressing room, while I was putting on my suit, changing from my track suit. He said: "the chairman would like you to see him with Chris Hughton". I said "OK" and then went into the players dressing room and told the boys: "I will always follow you. Do your best. Tonight, this was not good enough, I know you can do much better and I will always follow you and it has been great knowing you."

The players applauded me.

I then went up to see Daniel Levy and Sir Keith Mills. The first sentence I said was: "Fellows, let's call it a day."

Daniel told me that it had been a huge embarrassment for him and the club that the news had leaked out during the day. He told me that they had done everything to try to avoid it. They said they tried to stop a certain press man from releasing it before the game. I was even told that they thought the club must be bugged for it to have leaked. They said any information that was being dealt with had been embargoed, that no-one could have leaked that they knew about.

Daniel being embarrassed made me feel better. He said he regretted how it came out. If he'd sat me down eight weeks earlier and said: "We've got someone who can do better", that would have been okay.

There has been much said in the media about how angry I had got, and that there had been a heated row. Not true. Daniel is not like that. I am not like that. I can control myself. There have only been three or four times I couldn't control myself with the players, but I made it a rule that I never shouted at them. Yes, I admit there were a few times I got angry over the seasons. But if you shout all the time as a manger it doesn't work, the players stop listening and take no notice. In any case, I look serious, I look as though I am angry, and that's enough!

I hate the fact that I ended my career with defeat at White Hart Lane in Europe. We had never lost at home. Even in all the pre-season friendlies against some of the biggest names in the world like Inter Milan, Lyon and Boca Juniors, we had never lost. We won tournaments in South Africa, in France and must have played 24 games at this kind of level, which was evidence that we could play against the top European teams. But I could sense that night that something was wrong with the players virtually from the moment the game kicked off. My players were giving the opposition far too much space, they didn't seem to be giving that extra 10 per cent of commitment that they normally would do, and we lost in the last few minutes. I just had this feeling something was wrong.

Something very strange happened just one minute before the kick off that night. Berbatov came over to me and said: "Sorry boss! Come on!"

I thought to myself, whatever can he mean? It felt awkward. But

I was unsure what he meant. I thought that perhaps he was regretting what had happened in the previous match at Newcastle, or that he hadn't given me his best before, but it did not cross my mind that he and the rest of the players had already been told by friends who had been texting them that I had been sacked.

At St. James Park, a lot had been made in the media about Berbatov's attitude, that he didn't want to come on because he was sulking at being left on the bench. Well, when it came to the time I wanted to make a change I was out in my technical area and I looked over my shoulder to tell Berbatov to warm up. Normally Chris Hughton would tell the players to warm up, but not this time. However, he didn't seem that keen to do it. I turned my shoulder again and this time I looked him in the eye and told him: "come on, warm up" and he began to warm up. He never said he didn't want to come on, but that's how it has been perceived. But that was Berbatov, he always seemed reluctant to do anything. He was like it last year and it was the same this season. But I didn't take any notice of it. It was because he was an introverted character and the dressing room is made up of all sorts of characters. The point is that he is a gifted individual. He is like Johan Cruyff and I cannot put him any higher than that. Gifted, yes. But he is not a fighter. Perhaps you need others who are fighters to balance out the team.

So when he came up to me a minute before kick off in what turned out to be my last game, I thought he was apologising for what had been said about everything at Newcastle.

Everyone got it wrong. They said I stayed on the bench and didn't go to the touchline, but that was because the German bugger of a fourth official wouldn't let me! Spurs fans were singing my name, but they always sang my name, so I didn't think it was unusual. People say I was crying, but I swear I didn't know – it was probably a windy night. I was stressed because I didn't want to lose. But maybe the players had an idea. Of course there have been rumours about me, there had been rumours every day, so why should I listen to more rumours? I had been waiting so long, I thought it wasn't going to happen.

We all knew the club had been to Seville to see Ramos, but it looked as though he didn't want to take the job, or couldn't take it in the middle of the season and that he wasn't coming until the end of the season. Call me arrogant, but I didn't think the club would find anybody better than me. Not even someone like Jose Mourinho could have done better than me at this club under the circumstances. It was easy to be champions as manager of Chelsea, but when you look at our line up over the last two years, to finish fifth in successive seasons is something I don't believe he, or anyone else for that matter, could have managed at this club. And then when you think that for seven months we were in the top four, and only missed out in the last game of the season, when Arsenal finished fourth, that is one hell of an achievement.

Jermaine Jenas recalled how it affected the team, as well as Jol himself, "I remember speaking to him before the game because I was carrying an injury and his face was just blank, as if he was looking right through me. In the weeks leading up to that, you could tell something had changed within him. It was leaked in the papers that Spurs were speaking to Juande Ramos. We'd seen it, he had obviously seen it, so it was impossible to ignore. As players, we were trying to concentrate on doing our jobs – and we all liked Martin – but there's no doubt it was distracting."

A jovial character who liked to get his press conferences over with to focus on the more pressing issue of smoking cigarettes, Jol was hugely popular with the fans. Spurs supporters could sense the start of a revival, a rise in expectations, and the start of something very special. He had an affinity with the club and its traditions which was something that warmed him to fans, as he had supported Spurs as an eight-year-old back in his native Holland. He now looks back at his three years as Spurs manager when he says with affection, "I was always a Tottenham fan since I was eight with my brother, I had the shirt of Jimmy Greaves from the sixties. When I was manager, we lived in Chigwell and I was the only one who was left there in the end. Everybody else moved to Enfield, but I stuck with Chigwell. I've still got my house there, I don't know why but I can't bring myself to sell it. If I have a week off or my little girl has her holidays, we still visit. It's nice."

Having qualified for the 2007-08 UEFA Cup, Jol tempted Dutch legend Edgar Davids to the club as Spurs stepped up their pursuit of a top four finish and Champions League qualification. Darren Bent also arrived and was the most expensive signing of Jol's reign. One of Jol's first moves in the transfer market saw him raid Forest for the joint signings of Andy Reid and Michael Dawson. A focus on young English players was restored too, with Jermaine Jenas, Aaron Lennon and Tom Huddlestone all being brought in. One of Jol's final additions was a 16-year-old Danny Rose for just £1m. Yet capitulation to Arsenal in the 2006-07 League Cup semi-final summed up Jol's reign; under him the club never seemed to win the big games.

He was rewarded with a Porsche 911 by Levy for his exploits in Europe, which he secretly sold, but Jol fully aware that the Champions League was the Holy Grail. Jol never quite achieved the goal of Champions League football. He came pretty close. "Daniel and his vice-chairman Paul Kemsley were obsessed with the Champions League," said Jol. "Paul told me 'if you play in Europe, I will give you a BMW', so when we were in the UEFA Cup I was waiting for it and I think I got a watch from his driver instead. It was a nice watch, but I gave it to my nephew and I never asked about the BMW. Paul never turned up with the BMW, but maybe a year later when we qualified for Europe again, Daniel gave me a Porsche 911. That was nice, but the thing was I already had the same Porsche, so I secretly sold it a couple of months later. It didn't come with any of the papers, so I had to make an excuse to ask for them so I could sell it!"

The defining moment of Jol's reign was a first league victory over Chelsea in 16 years. Dawson and Lennon got the goals. The Dutchman's first official game in charge, a 5-4 defeat to Arsenal in which Noureddine Naybet opened the goal fest with a volley, became the first match in Premier League history to have nine different scorers.

The writing was on the wall after a run of defeats capped by a 3-1 loss to Arsenal; the sense in the boardroom was that Jol had taken the club as far as he could. Jol's position was untenable from the moment members of the Tottenham board had been pictured in Spain with the then-Sevilla boss Juande Ramos. Few will need reminding how big an error of judgement that decision turned out to be; Ramos took over within days but was gone a year later.

"You know I will never say anything negative about Spurs," Jol said of his time at White Hart Lane, "it was like a rose garden and you never spit in your own garden."

The closest Jol got to achieving Levy's dream was in 2006, when Tottenham had spent the majority of the season in the top four, but slipped to fifth on the final day thanks to a defeat against West Ham United after a number of players had fallen ill with food-poisoning. Asked for his version of events of 'lasagne-gate', Jol said: "On the morning of the game, at 4.30am, the doctor phoned me and said 'we've got a problem, the players are ill'. It was obvious something went off. People were going to the doctor and all sorts, it was very strange, but I don't want to blame anything like that. It was never easy to go to West Ham, so I don't want to look for an excuse. I can remember Michael Carrick was ill and he still played, but it's too long ago to worry about. We were the best of the rest at the time and that was good."

Jol holds no grudge over his exit. He still considers Spurs "my club" and he accepted an apology from former club secretary John Alexander, who had been pictured with Kemsley and Juande Ramos a few months before the Spaniard replaced Jol. Describing how he got the top job at Spurs after Santini quit, Jol said: "When Daniel made the offer to me and my manager, Mino Raiola, he said 'you will have to take it or leave it because we have five managers at the gate waiting to be manager'. Mino said 'ok, we take it'. Five months later, I went to speak to Freddy Shepherd's son about Newcastle and Paul Kemsley was in the room next to us at the Dorchester Hotel. Kemsley probably thought 'what the f--- is Martin doing, he's talking to Newcastle' because Shepherd was his friend. So then they had to give me a better contract, so Mino was right. Daniel had to give me what I wanted in the end.

*Martn Jol with his head in his hands on the night he was
infamously fired at half-time*

That was nice."

Damien Comolli was appointed Director of Football to work
with Jol at Tottenham but is not remembered fondly. "This Damien
Comolli was very young and I couldn't get on with him. He came
into my dressing-room before games and stood against the wall
in team meetings. I would say 'what are you doing? F--- off', so
he had to leave the room. It wasn't a great relationship. Comolli
was a smooth talker, I was a lot older and it was not easy. But
Daniel believed in that structure and he had to take a decision. He
eventually said to me 'let's call it a day' and I had felt it coming, so
I don't feel badly towards him."

Jol spent a successful season in Germany with Hamburg
before, in 2009, taking over at Ajax, where he had a big hand in the
development of three of Tottenham's best players under Pochettino.
Jan Vertonghen was converted from a left-back and midfielder into
a centre-back at Ajax. Jol put Toby Alderweireld in the team as a
regular. "Toby and Jan played together for me, one was 20 and the
other was 21. We had an unbelievable season, we only conceded

four goals in the whole season at home. Christian Eriksen made his debut with me, he was always playing with Frank de Boer in the Under-18s. He was 17 and I took him from the youth and he didn't even play for the Under-21s. I put him straight into the first team. I think Christian is now the most influential midfielder of his type in England. When he is not playing, you get a different Spurs. He makes them tick. He wants the ball all the time, he has so much confidence."

Having resigned from his job at Ajax after 18 months, Jol returned to England with Fulham and revealed how he accused Levy of leaving him no chance to improve on an encouraging first season after the Cottagers had finished ninth. "Clint Dempsey was scoring my goals and Mousa Dembele was my best player," said Jol. "Tottenham came in and I phoned Daniel and said 'are you f----- me over for the second time now?' But Daniel never loses his temper, he just said 'it's business'. It's funny now, but at the time I was... do you know a better word for it than f-----?"

9: BILL NICHOLSON

OCTOBER 1958 to SEPTEMBER 1974

"NOW THEN," THE GREAT MAN SAID EYEING the youthful Spurs correspondent of the now long defunct *Tottenham Weekly Herald*, whose offices on Tottenham High Road were a clichéd stone's throw away from the White Hart Lane ground, "when would you like to see me?"

"As I have to write about the team each week with a Wednesday deadline and early Thursday morning if there is a midweek game, could I see you every Monday morning?" I said eagerly.

There were a few seconds silence and a touch of bewilderment seemed to come over one of the most authoritative football managers of all-time before the Yorkshireman smiled and leaned over, in a way one could imagine he did when confiding some tactical point to Danny Blanchflower or Jimmy Greaves. Dear old Bill Nicholson was about to give me an important instruction, and I had better make sure I understood every word of it!

Finally Bill said, with slight amazement, "Your predecessor saw me once a season!"

Slightly aghast at having offended the great man, I was struck dumb and there were a few seconds of embarrassing silence, which seemed more like half an hour, as I realised that I had put my foot in it, in my very first meeting with the Mr Tottenham himself before Mr Nicholson thought again and said, "Come and see me Monday morning before training, here in my office, and we shall see how we go, but remember, once a season your predecessor saw me, and he was lucky he got that time once a year!"

So the next Monday morning before training I was there bright and early and I carried on turning up bright and early for the next *seven* years! During that time Bill Nicholson welcomed me into his inner sanctum and spoke to me on average for around 15 minutes as he gave me a comprehensive run down on just about everything that went on inside the club, except of course those matters he wished to keep to himself, and as the years went by he trusted me more and began to confide in me more.

One day I turned up around five minutes late for one of Bill's now well established Monday morning briefings. Usually I was always sitting outside his office waiting patiently to be called, I always made a point of being punctual. I knew how much he detested anyone turning up late. As a stickler for punctuality, I think he liked the fact I was always on time, if not always early. However, not this time. I started to make up some sort of excuse about transport, a genuine reason for my late show, and (to this day I've no idea why I said it, perhaps out of nervousness and guilt) I said that the one and only watch I owned had stopped, and that had also thrown me.

The next Monday morning I came for my weekly chat in his office and before I could say a word Bill told me that he was upset that I was late the previous week, and even more perturbed that my only watch had stopped. He reached into the top draw of his desk and pulled out a handsome looking case. He handed it to me.

"Now, never tell me your watch has stopped again!"

Inside was a solid gold watch inscribed to Bill from AC Milan. Mr Nicholson had been presented with it by the crack Italian club before a big European tie. I didn't know what to say, apart from a very bumbling "thank you, thank you very much".

Often I would work late at the *Herald* offices and walk along the High Road to catch my bus and whenever I looked up at the White Hart Lane offices I would see the bare light bulb still on in Bill's office which fronted onto the main road. He lived and breathed Spurs and spent more time in that office than he did at home.

On 29th August, 1974, Bill Nicholson resigned as manager, ending a remarkable association with the club which stretched back over thirty-eight years to 1936 when he joined the club as a young player of seventeen. He was a huge success as a player during a 16 year career from 1938, in a spell rudely interrupted by the war, before becoming coach and later manager.

Not long after he retired I went round to his humble home where his wife made me tea and cake. I had been pestering him about writing his autobiography, insisting that he should chronicle his life. I have one last copy left of that book signed by Bill and the entire Double team who turned out for the launch of the book.

Bill Nicholson's CV at his beloved Spurs makes pretty impressive reading. He was full back in the 'Push and Run' team which won the Second Division and First Division titles in successive seasons between 1949 and 1951. As manager he won his first match 10–4 against Everton at White Hart Lane in October 1958. He went on to become the club's most successful manager, guiding the team to the historic League and FA Cup 'Double' in 1960-61, the FA Cup in 1962 and 1967, the Football League Cup in 1971 and 1973 and the European Cup Winners' Cup in 1963 as the first British club to win a European trophy and the UEFA Cup in 1972.

Bill Nick dedicated his whole life to Tottenham Hotspur, and although the actual ground has never been in White Hart Lane, but in Tottenham High Road, his dedication to the club was such that he lived less than a mile from the ground in White Hart Lane itself in a humble terraced house.

The 1974-75 season had started disappointingly with four straight defeats; the opening game at home to Ipswich Town, at Manchester City in midweek and at newly promoted Carlisle United the following Saturday. All three defeats had been by a single goal and the goal which Martin Peters scored against Manchester City at White Hart Lane the following Wednesday was their first of the season but Spurs lost 1–2. City had taken the lead early in the second half. Peters brought the scores level five minutes later but a very late goal in the final seconds by City condemned Tottenham. Nicholson announced his shock resignation the following day.

He had found defeat in the previous season's UEFA Cup Final in Rotterdam against Feyenoord extremely stressful. Going into the second leg level at 2–2, there was rioting among the fans and ugly scenes on the terraces during the match had affected the proud

Yorkshireman. He was also finding it increasingly difficult to relate to the 'modern' player, especially ordinary ones demanding massive salaries and having been unable to strengthen his side during the summer, he decided it was time to step down.

Writing in his autobiography, 'Glory Glory, My Life with Spurs', which I co-wrote with my *Daily Mail* colleague at the time Brian Scovell, Bill Nicholson commented on his resignation, "Numerous reasons were put forward as to why I resigned in 1974, including contract disputes with players, the failure to buy new players, the first defeat in a Cup Final under my managership when we lost to Feyenoord on that disturbing night in Rotterdam, my trouble with Martin Chivers and the League defeats at the start of the season. All of them may have been contributory factors but the simple truth was that I was burned out. I resigned because I sensed I needed a long rest, I had no more to offer. It was really nothing to do with Martin Chivers or anyone else."

The Board and the players tried unsuccessfully to persuade him to change his mind, he agreed to stay on until his replacement was appointed, and although asked by the directors to help them find his successor, he was actually not consulted even though he had discussed the opportunity of hiring Johnny Giles and recruiting Terry Butcher.

Mr Nicholson set such high standards that successive Spurs' managers have found him a hard act to follow. John Pratt, quoted in, 'Mr Tottenham Hotspur - Memories of a Spurs Legend' by Steve E Hale, published in 2005, after Bill's death said of that August day in 1974, "It was such a shock. We all thought that Bill would be at Tottenham forever." While Jimmy Greaves said of his former boss, "His legacy is to have left forever something that all Spurs teams and staff should aspire to: that is to play football in a correct, honourable and entertaining manner."

Bill Nicholson will be remembered for the style of that Double team, and for the glories in Europe, and he might well have been the first to deliver the European Cup to these shores, after buying Jimmy Greaves to add greater goalscoring power to his already fabulous Double team.

Manchester City might have cursed VAR as Spurs marched into the Champions League semi-finals after an epic encounter in one of the most thrilling European ties ever under Mauricio Pochettino last season but had VAR existed in 1962 Spurs might have been the first British team to win the European Cup. Talk about balancing up your luck over the course of a season, for Spurs it has been a wait of an incredible 57 years to get their slice of a referee's verdict in the premier European tournament. It's pretty certain that Pep Guardiola and City won't have to wait another 60 years for their next crack at the Final!

Sitting in the living room of Bill Nicholson's humble terrace in White Hart Lane working on his book, he related the story of their momentous European Cup semi-final against a Eusebio-inspired Benfica when he was convinced that the officials got it badly wrong in Lisbon's Stadium of Light in disallowing at least one of two goals from Jimmy Greaves and Bobby Smith for offside and then suffering at the hands of the same dodgy referring decisions back at White Hart Lane. Jimmy Greaves reckons he was robbed not once but twice over the course of their two leg epic encounter with Eusebio's team; the 'Black Pearl' was challenging Pele as the greatest player of the era at the time.

Nicholson recalls the lovely sunny day in Lisbon, the packed stadium, and that his team were so good having won The Double the previous season, that they were not the slightest bit intimidated by the remarkable atmosphere. "We had two 'goals' disallowed by the Swiss referee Muellet, the first when Greaves beat a full-back and put the ball into the net only to be given offside and the second when Greaves pulled the ball back for Smith to 'score'. Greaves was certain that he was ahead of Smith when he passed, which meant that it was impossible for him to be offside. In the inquest afterwards the referring decisions were blamed for our defeat, but I said: 'We gave away two vital goals because three players in a row made stupid mistakes.'

European Cup Semi-final, First Leg - 21st Match 1962
Benfica 3 Tottenham Hotspur 1 - attendance:- 86.000

BENFICA: Costa Pereira; Joao, Angelo, Cavem, Germano, Cruz, Augusto, Eusebio, Aguas, Coluna, Simoes.

SPURS: Brown; Baker, Henry, Marchi, Norman, Mackay, Greaves, White, R Smith, Blanchflower, Jones.

On March 21st 1962, in the first leg of the Semi-final, Spurs had fallen behind after only five minutes when Bill Brown punched the ball away from Coluna. Unfortunately, the ball ran loose to Simoes, then 18 but a future star for the Eagles, and lobbed the ball back for Aguas to score. A moment later the 500 Spurs fans in Stadium da Luz thought Greaves had equalised but Jimmy's disgust the goal was disallowed. Augusto fired Benfica two ahead in the 19th minute but in the 54th minute Spurs reduced the arrears when Blanchflower floated a ball over for Smith to thump home. Benfica regained control of the tie when Augusto nodded the ball in to give Benfica a 3-1 lead. Spurs should have reduced the arrears in the dying moments, but despite two Benfica defenders actually on the goal-line, the referee decided Smith was offside!
Wednesday 21st March, 1962

European Cup Semi-final, Second Leg, 5th April, 1962
Tottenham Hotspur 2 Benfica 1 - Attendance:- 64,448

SPURS: Brown; Baker, Henry, Blanchflower, Norman, Mackay, Medwin, White, R Smith, Greaves, Jones.

BENFICA: Costa Pereira; Joao, Angelo, Cavem, Germano, Cruz, Augusto, Eusebio, Aguas, Coluna, Simoes.

The second leg was a pulsating occasion played on a Thursday night. The old stadium echoed to the 'Glory, Glory!' anthem. Much is made of the acoustics created by the "Dortmund" style Wall of 17,500 fans behind the goal in their new near £1 billion new super stadium, but the old Lane had its moments back in the 60s.

Nicholson recalled: "A new sound was heard in English football in the 1961-2 season. It was the hymn 'Glory, glory Hallelujah' being sung by 60,000 at White Hart Lane in our European Cup matches. I do not know how it started or who started it, but it took over the ground like a religious feeling. No congregation at the biggest church assembly in the country could possibly match the noise that was to be heard off the Tottenham High Road. Danny Blanchflower said of the supporters of that time; 'they were showing their faith and were not to be denied.'

"Liverpool's Kop may have equalled it with 'You'll Never Walk Alone', but I doubt whether any ground has ever echoed to a greater volume of noise in the south than White Hart Lane in the early sixties. The sound went all around the stadium. It was the Tottenham hymn and it frightened the opposing sides from Europe - well, most of them. The exception was the Portuguese champion team Benfica which put us out of the European Cup in the semi-final."

Nicholson had gone to watch Real Madrid win their quarter-final tie against Standard Liege 4-0 to virtually assure themselves of a place in the final but Bill came away convinced that had they beaten Benfica, which he felt was achievable by his outstanding team, then they would have won the Final. "I believe that, but for some marginal refereeing decisions that went against us, we would have qualified to play Real in the final and would have gone on to win."

Nicholson could never have imagined mobile phones, the internet, electric cars, let alone VAR but his team's rightful place in the Final was denied because the technology was light years away that would have righted the wrongs of those incredible nights against Benfica.

In the second leg, Spurs fell behind in the 15th minute when Aguas strode through the defence, it was an early set back reminiscent of the way the tie went against Manchester City went almost 60 years later. Spurs, though, were by far the dominant team, and thought they had equalised in the 23rd minute. Smith flicked the ball on to Greaves, who waltzed through the Benfica defence, only to see the goal disallowed for offside. The referee awarded a goal but the linesman held up his flag. In the 35th minute Spurs equalised as Smith dragged them back into the game. Two minutes after the break, Coluna sent White flying in the penalty area and Blanchflower struck home the penalty. Spurs needed one more goal to force a replay in Brussels, two to win it outright.

Spurs powered forward relentlessly in search of the goal and after several chances, the mighty Dave Mackay raced forward, his shot was goal bound, fans were celebrating an amazing come-back when the ball struck the cross bar and bounced harmlessly into the crowd behind the Park Lane goal.

Nicholson recalled: "The return leg at White Hart Lane on 5 April 1962 was described by David Miller as 'the most electrifying ninety minutes of European football I have ever seen on an English ground.' Thousands of fans were locked out and Bela Guttmann, the Benfica manager, was so worried that his players might be affected by the atmosphere that he declined to send them out on to the field before kick-off to warm up.

"Bela was an interesting character. A member of the 1924 Hungarian Olympic side, he spent the war years in a concentration camp and coached sides to championship success in his native Hungary and in Italy, Brazil and Portugal. He could speak five languages, including English, and he reminded me of the Italian coach Vittorio Pozzo, who led Italy to success in the 1934 and 1938 World Cups. Pozzo was also a linguist. Guttman was sixty-two when he came to Tottenham and he used all his wiles to ensure that his team survived one of the most difficult challenges of its history.

"On his arrival he told journalists that he was worried about the aggression of Dave Mackay and Bobby Smith and said he hoped the referee, Aage Poulsen, a Dane, would not let them get away with any excesses. However, I do not think that was a factor in our elimination from the competition.

"There were many free-kicks against us but we lost because the luck didn't go with us. Three times we struck the woodwork to Benfica's once and for a third time in the tie we had a goal disallowed for offside. The referee seemed willing to accept that

*Bill always told me he disliked any paperwork that came
with the job, his real office was the training ground..*

Greaves had scored a good goal, but the linesman raised his flag."

Pictures that night showed the linesman racing to try to keep up with the speed of Greaves and was well behind the play with his flag raised while he was still sprinting! He was definitely not in line with play, and those infamous lines on a VAR assessment would have shown Greaves was well onside!

"Aguas, a tall, elegant centre-forward, scored after fifteen minutes to make the aggregate 1-4," Bill continued, "John

White laid on a goal for Smith in the thirty-eighth minute and Blanchflower converted a penalty in the forty-ninth. With forty-one minutes remaining we were 3-4 down and perhaps we should have at least forced a play-off. It was said that in the deafening noise and throbbing passion, our players panicked and played in a style that was alien to them, thumping the ball upfield at every opportunity. Maurice Norman was moved to centre-forward to take on Germano in the air. I do not believe we were wrong to play that way. It was how the game went. Benfica defended with desperation and there were many near misses.

"But afterwards we knew, and Bela Guttman, must have known too, that Benfica, the European champion team, was lucky to survive. Benfica went on to win in Amsterdam against Real with Puskas on the losing side despite scoring a hat-trick."

Jimmy Greaves knew it too, "I thought it was a good one. I ran between two Benfica players before shooting. This is twice I have been 'done' in the European Cup. I don't think anyone will ever be able to change my view of that. There were defenders all round me. Bobby slotted the ball through and I went between at least two defenders before shooting past Costa Pereira, the Benfica goalkeeper. I really thought that goal would be the one that would put us through to the final. The disappointment of that defeat was immense. I felt a little guilty because I missed some great chances after that, but I don't think it was mean to be my year."

Nicholson was convinced that it wouldn't be long before his Super Spurs team would win the European Cup, but here we are, nearly 60 years later years later and last season was by far the closest Spurs have come to winning 'old big ears'.

No one would be more pleased if Spurs had gone on to win the Final as Bill Nicholson who I am sure is looking down on the wonderment of VAR.

BILL NICHOLSON QUOTES

"It's magnificent to be in Europe, and this club – a club like Tottenham Hotspur – if we're not in Europe…. we're nothing. We're nothing."

"Naturally I'm a Tottenham man. So far as football is concerned, it means almost everything, doesn't it really? Because I can reflect back to being a player with, and manager of some of the finest players that have ever been in the game."

"I always said that it was an honour to serve Tottenham Hotspur and I feel the same every time I walk back into the stadium."

"It's been my life, Tottenham Hotspur, and I love the club."

10: GLENN HODDLE

GLENN HODDLE IS ONE OF MY ALL-TIME SPURS heroes. What a player! And all Spurs fans wanted him to be as successful as a Spurs manager when the club appointed him as their new manager on Friday March 30, 2001 replacing the sacked George Graham. Glenn took the job just four days after resigning as boss of Southampton. Hoddle agreed a long-term contract appointing his long-time assistant, John Gorman, after the club dismissed Graham's number two Stewart Houston. Speaking at a media conference at White Hart Lane, Hoddle was delighted to have "returned home".

"It's emotional and exciting," he said. "I've spent many years here and the supporters have given me a superb reception. I walked through the gates of this club at age eight as a supporter and left when I was 29. That's a huge part of my life."

The former England boss insisted there had been no doubts on his part. "I don't feel guilty," he said of his controversial departure from The Dell. "The timing was right to come back. It's a fantastic club. I'm very surprised to be here and when I was offered the chance to talk to Spurs it was something I wanted to pursue. There was only one club I would have left Southampton for and that was Tottenham Hotspur Football Club."

Hoddle had high hopes but it was important to plan for the long-term. "The potential is there to do well and there's lots of hard work to be done. The fact that the contract is five years means the club are looking to the future. We want to win the Premiership, of course we do, and that is my ultimate goal, but it's early doors to be talking about that.

"Spurs have always had a style. In an ideal world that is what we want but you must have a balance. The game has changed since the 1960s and you have to change with it. Tottenham didn't have to prove anything to me and there is talent in the squad, no doubt

Yours truly and a couple of Spurs legends.

about it."

Hoddle, who played over 350 times for Tottenham, winning the UEFA Cup in 1984 and back-to-back FA Cups, guided the side to a League Cup final against Blackburn a year later. Spurs finished ninth and tenth in successive seasons under Hoddle before he was sacked in September 2003. He had more than 100 games in charge but could do no better than a ninth-placed finish in his first full season. After a poor start to the 2003–04 season and with no wins in four games, a 3-1 defeat to, of all teams, Southampton proved too much for Levy.

In hindsight Glenn always felt inhibited with David Pleat in the role as technical director, and felt hampered in some of the signings he pursued. He always fancied another crack at the Spurs job and it almost came about when he was among those tipped to replace Andre Villas-Boas; he was more than willing to return, even on a short term basis but technical co-ordinator Tim Sherwood was placed in temporary charge after Villas-Boas' 17 months reign came to an end after a 5-0 thrashing by Liverpool that left them seventh in the table. Former England manager Fabio Capello, Swansea boss Michael Laudrup and Tottenham's current technical director Franco Baldini were all linked with replacing the Portuguese but Hoddle enjoyed fruitful talks with Daniel Levy, and it all looked highly promising before the Spurs chairman changed his mind overnight and opted for Sherwood instead.

Hoddle had not managed since he left Wolves in June 2006 and that probably tipped the balance against him. Having turned down other offers to return to the game, including the chance to take charge of the Ukraine national side, Glenn has also opened an academy in Spain which focuses on keeping released players in the game.

Former Spurs and England striker Gary Lineker tweeted at the time of the rumours, "Would love to see Glenn Hoddle given another chance at this level, has a brilliant football mind." Hoddle, though, had unfinished business not only at Spurs but with England too. He said he would be willing to answer the call to either Spurs or England, but seems more than content with life as a TV pundit, and we all wish him well after his very serious heart scare while working as a BT Sport pundit.

Glenn opted to 'dip his toe in the water' as he put it when asked by his old friend Harry Redknapp to help him with coaching duties at QPR, but that didn't last long before Redknapp parted company with the west London club. Glenn did enjoy getting back on the training ground but since his heart operation that now seems highly unlikely.

Former midfielder Sherwood, who played 93 league games for the club, was only expected to be in charge on a temporary basis as the club sought their fourth manager in six years. It was a huge shock, not least to Hoddle, when Levy decided to appoint Sherwood on a permanent basis, a man with no previous management experience. Sherwood signed an 18-month deal, but failed to reach his second season as the club exercised a break clause in the contract. He won 14 of his 28 games in charge as Spurs finished a respectable sixth, 10 points behind Arsenal in fourth.

A 5-1 home defeat to eventual champions Manchester City and a 4-0 thrashing at Chelsea saw Sherwood question the commitment of a number of his players. He always claimed the uncertainty over his position was making the job harder and, as the season drew to a close, even his players started suggesting Sherwood's tenure was coming to an end. Midfielder Sandro, who had fallen out of favour under Sherwood, told ESPN Brazil he was expecting a new man to be in charge at the start of the new campaign and he was proven correct.

"It is obviously a massive wrench to leave a club of the stature of Tottenham Hotspur, a club very close to my heart," Sherwood said. Levy said on the club's website: "We appointed Tim mid-season as someone who knew both the players and the club. We agreed an 18-month contract with a break clause at the end of the season and we have now exercised that option. Since appointing Tim as assistant first team coach in 2008 and then as technical co-ordinator in 2010 and head of football development in 2012, we have been supportive of him during football management changes throughout that period. On behalf of the club, I should like to state our thanks for all his efforts during his years with us. We wish him great success in his managerial career. Moving forward, now the season is over, we shall embark on the process of finding a new head coach. We have a talented squad and exciting young players coming through. We need to build on this season, develop our potential and inspire the kind of performances that we associate with our great club.'

Sherwood actually won 50% of games in his short time as manager, but humiliating defeats by Liverpool, Manchester City, Chelsea and West Ham meant his tenure was always likely to be short. Mauricio Pochettino took over from Sherwood, and became the longest running boss in recent years until Daniel Levy eventually sacked him too. Since Levy arrived in 2000, nine managers have sat in the Spurs hot-seat on a permanent basis, plus a couple of caretakers, adding up to eleven different men in the Spurs dugout during Levy's near two-decade reign. Jacques Santini had the shortest reign in the club's history, the Frenchman lasted just 13 games before leaving citing personal problems despite being in fourth position after an unbeaten start to the campaign.

Hoddle spoke about his TV studio cardiac arrest when his heart stopped for a minute in the BT Sport studio on his 61st birthday. Robbie Savage yelled for help as sound engineer Simon Daniels raced to Glenn's aid and had to break seven of his ribs as he desperately pounded his chest to bring him back to life.

Glenn revealed: "My heart stopped for at least 60 seconds. I was gone. The engineer ran to me and brought me back to life. I wouldn't be here if not for him. It just wasn't my time to go. Robbie and I had been playing the keepy-uppy game at the end of the programme. Robbie said that after the credits rolled I was just at the moment of volleying the ball back to him when I fell backwards and smashed my head on the floor. It's ironic that if I had died, the last thing I would have done on this earth was kick a ball. What a way to go! It could have happened on live TV. The timing of everything on the day was incredible. Robbie thought I was messing around with him when I fell to the floor. We had been having banter. Then he stopped laughing and thought I might have swallowed my tongue. But he soon realised something very serious had happened. He couldn't do anything, so started shouting for help. Thank God first-aider Simon was nearby and got to me so quickly. If he had been in the toilet, or left the studio, or not on duty, I would not be here to tell my story. He performed chest compressions and fitted a defibrillator on my chest to keep me alive. Simon is a mild-mannered guy and was apologetic afterwards because something kicked in during the emergency and he was ordering everyone about. He told strangers 'Do this, do that'. He is a volunteer policeman and was embarrassed. It goes without saying if my cardiac arrest had struck on the golf course, or when I was watching Spurs play in the Netherlands a few days earlier, I'd be a goner."

Hoddle is now one of the country's leading TV pundits, and on the appointment of Mourinho he felt that Christian Eriksen would not fit in with the new managers plans. "I'm not sure Mourinho and Eriksen is a great fit anyway. Eriksen has made it pretty clear he wants a move away from Tottenham and I can see Mourinho not picking him regularly.

"Mourinho demands total respect in the dressing room and will install a bit of fear in his players. He doesn't suffer fools and he knows what he wants. And if players aren't prepared to buy into that he'll leave them out. Don't get me wrong, Mourinho isn't afraid of flair players, but an Eriksen would never be the cornerstone of his team."

In May 2004 Glenn was inducted into the Spurs Hall of Fame, and at the event John Motson asked for a message to the current board and said "Get rid of this PLC lark, make it a football club again!"

11: TERRY VENABLES

TERRY VENABLES ARRIVED FROM BARCELONA at a difficult time for the club both financially and on the pitch. He galvanised the team and led them to third place behind perennial champions Liverpool in 1989-90 and signed quality players like Paul Gascoigne and Gary Lineker. The two prominent and exciting England players would have made a formidable force with Chris Waddle but Waddle had been sold to Marseille in 1989, the same summer as Lineker arrived. That summer all three players would star in England's World Cup adventure in Italy and returned as national heroes as football leapt from the back page to the front page.

Despite these star names and the Terry's success in guiding Spurs to victory in the 1991 FA Cup, the club was still in financial peril, although then chairman Irving Scholar always said that the financial issues were manageable. Eventually Venables brought in Alan Sugar to devise a rescue plan but their falling out brought further stress to the club with court issues and supporter opinion split. In the dug out Venables was a genius, but he was a flawed businessman. In a statement from the Department of Trade and Industry, Venables had reached a settlement with its lawyers, agreeing to be banned from any directorship, or virtually any other relationship with a commercial operation, for seven years. Accepting 19 charges of serious misconduct, all of which he had strenuously denied for the previous four years, Venables also agreed to pay half a million pounds of the DTI's costs. Three weeks earlier Venables' friend and business partner, Eddie Ashby, completed a four month prison sentence for breach of the bankruptcy laws.

Panorama reporter Martin Bashir described El Tel as a "loveable rogue" in the English tradition of Minder. He had charm and charisma but while he was investigated for dubious business practises, Venables was one of the managerial greats, achieving success at both club and international level. England's Euro '96 performance earned Venables national acclaim, but he walked away at the end of the tournament to fight a legal battle surrounding his business interests.

Terry built his coaching reputation in his early spells with Crystal Palace and Queens Park Rangers, having played for both clubs in the latter part of a career that saw him earn honours at every single level for England. His playing career began at Chelsea, where, having come up through the junior ranks, he made over 200 appearances in midfield and helped the Blues to victory in the 1965 League Cup. After six seasons at Stamford Bridge, Terry moved to Tottenham where he spent three years before moving back west to join QPR, and then south to join Palace.

Having retired as a player, Terry took on the manager's job at Selhurst Park - taking over from Malcolm Allison - and guided the club into the top flight, as champions of Division Two, in the 1978-79 season. He then returned to take charge at QPR, and took the Superhoops to the FA Cup final in 1982, and to the Second Division title the following season. His success in charge of the two London clubs attracted the interest of a number of clubs in England and Europe, and in 1984 Terry became the manager of Spanish giants Barcelona, then in something of a slump. Terry won the La Liga title (the club's first since 1974) in his first season and his incredible success and popularity earned him the nickname 'El Tel'. With English clubs banned from European competition he also lured some of Britain's best players to Catalonia during his three-year spell in Spain with the acquisition of the likes of Mark Hughes, Gary Lineker and Steve Archibald. His success continued the following season as he won the League Cup but his reign in Spain never quite recovered from Barcelona's failure to beat Steaua Bucharest in the European Cup final in Seville. Before 70,000 Catalans they couldn't score in normal time or extra time and then missed all their penalties in the resulting shoot-out and lost it 2-0.

Terry returned to London in 1987 to manage another former club, Tottenham Hotspur. Spurs chairman Irving Scholar had sacked David Pleat with a particularly heavy heart. The fact that

Pleat's personal problems came to a breaking point at the time that Venables was being replaced by Barcelona was merely coincidental. Pleat had taken the club to third place in the league and was the first Spurs boss to lose a Wembley final when they were beaten by Coventry in the FA Cup Final. Pleat had become the nearly man at Spurs, he had come so close to glory, but never quite got over the line.

With Lineker and Gascoigne in the side, Venables led Spurs to glory in the FA Cup where – despite Gazza's infamous self-induced injury – they beat Brian Clough's Nottingham Forest at Wembley in 1991. A falling-out with the then Spurs chairman Alan Sugar led to Terry's departure from White Hart Lane just a month after the FA Cup triumph, and it was with England, three years later, that he returned to management – becoming President of the LMA.

Under Venables England went all the way to the semi-finals of the Euro '96 tournament and his team's 4–1 destruction of Holland in the opening phase remains one of the finest by the national team in modern times. They also beat auld enemies Scotland but were a little fortunate to beat Spain on penalties before losing the same way to Germany, who went on to beat the Czechs in the final.

Spells at Portsmouth and Crystal Palace followed for Terry, as well as a short period in charge of the Australian national team, who were desperately unlucky not to qualify for their first World Cup in 1998 under 'El Tel'. Two years later Terry got his first taste of life in the FA Carling Premiership and it was very much at the sharp end with Middlesbrough, alongside Bryan Robson. His remit was to save the club from another quick return to Division One, and once more he was ultimately successful. Terry decided his business interests and media work could not allow him the time to take up a permanent role on Teesside, and he continued to work as a pundit on ITV; seen particularly during the 2002 World Cup.

Venables was then appointed manager of Leeds United on July 8, 2002. After his spell at Leeds, Venables returned to the international scene with England assisting Steve McClaren. Terry has since retired from football and runs a boutique hotel in Spain with his wife.

12: KEITH BURKINSHAW

KEITH BURKINSHAW IS ONE OF TOTTENHAM Hotspur's most successful managers. He served at White Hart Lane from 1976 to 1984, winning two FA Cups and the UEFA Cup. The FA Cup triumphs were in successive seasons, 1981 and 1982, in an era of Spurs greats which included Burkinshaw's key signings of Argentine World Cup winners Osvaldo Ardiles and Ricardo Villa. The UEFA Cup win came over R.S.C. Anderlecht in 1984 which proved to be Keith's final game in charge.

He was a coach at Newcastle United from 1968 until 1975 when he was sacked as part of a cost-cutting exercise when Terry Neill appointed him First Team Coach for Tottenham. In the summer of 1976 Neill resigned to become manager of Arsenal when the unassuming Burkinshaw was appointed his replacement. Spurs were relegated but the Board stood by him. Spurs made a good start to their first season in Division Two since May 1950 with an emerging Glenn Hoddle, a young Neil McNab and Keith Osgood. Spurs lost the title but managed to get the vital point they needed at Southampton in the final game of the season for promotion; their goal average was superior to Brighton's solely because of a 9-0 thrashing of Bristol Rovers the previous October.

During the close season, the World Cup was held in Argentina. Within days of that competition concluding, Spurs sensationally signed two members of the winning World Cup squad, Osvaldo Ardiles and Ricardo Villa, plus a centre-half from Fulham, John Lacy. Villa scored on his debut at Nottingham Forest, but it was Ardiles who began to forge a partnership in midfield with the maturing Hoddle. There was a spectacular 7-0 thrashing by Liverpool, where Tommy Smith was heard to dismiss Ardiles as a fancy Dan who would disappear when the winter months came, but Spurs enjoyed a good FA Cup run to the 6th Round, and finished the season in

11th place.

The following season saw them slip down the table but another good run in the Cup saw them reach the 6th Round again. Probably the high point of that season was winning at Old Trafford, when Glenn Hoddle was forced to replace Aleksic in goal and Ardiles scored the only goal of the match seconds from the end of extra time.

In the summer of 1980 Burkinshaw signed Steve Archibald and Garth Crooks to form a new striker partnership. The pair gelled from the start and they scored the majority of the goals over the season. That season Spurs returned to Wembley for the first time since 1967 for the Centenary Cup final against Manchester City. Villa was awful in the first match and was substituted midway through the second half by which time Tommy Hutchison had put City ahead and it looked as though Spurs were about to lose a proud record of never having lost a Wembley final. But late on, Spurs won a free-kick and from it, Hoddle equalised, with a wicked deflection off Hutchison, who thus scored for both teams!

In the replay Spurs were the better side, Villa firing them ahead after only five minutes and apart from a short spell where the Mancunians equalised and led, Crooks equalised midway through the second half and then Galvin was running down the left wing, almost lazily. He slipped the ball to Villa, who dodged round one City defender after another, drew Corrigan and slipped the ball over him before turning and racing to

Keith Burkinshaw with the trophy he made his own in the early 80s.

where Burkinshaw sat applauding.

Burkinshaw was not happy because Spurs had only finished 14th in the League. Just before the start of the season Spurs bought Gary Mabbutt from Bristol Rovers, despite the fact he was diabetic and needed regular injections of insulin. The side set off on what was to be a long, gruelling season with an appearance at Wembley against Aston Villa in the Charity Shield which was drawn 2-2, Mark Falco, deputising for the injured Crooks, scoring two great goals. In the Cup Winners' Cup for the first time since 1967, Spurs made good progress until they were drawn against Barcelona in the Semi-Final. Roberts scored a vital goal in the first leg at Tottenham, but they crashed in Spain, losing 1-0. In the League Cup they returned to Wembley, only to lose to Liverpool 3-1 in extra time, having come within four minutes of winning the final. The League slipped beyond their reach when they had to play 18 League matches between the beginning of March and the end of the season, Spurs eventually finished 4th. But Spurs returned to Wembley again beating Queen's Park Rangers in the Cup Final after Terry Fenwick, then playing for QPR, had struck to force injury time after Hoddle had put Spurs ahead. In the replay a Hoddle penalty gave Spurs the win that gave them the Cup after Roberts had been upended. But Ardiles and Villa were not at Wembley with Tottenham as both had gone because of the outbreak of war between the UK and Argentina over the Falklands.

Season 1982-83 saw Spurs set off on another four pronged assault. They lost possession of the Charity Shield to Liverpool, who beat them 1-0 at Wembley and were knocked out of the League Cup by Burnley, who crushed them 4-1 and lost 2-0 at Everton in the FA Cup. Their interest in Europe ended when a Karl-Heinz Rummeneigge inspired Bayern Munich side beat them 4-1 in Munich after a draw at Tottenham.

But changes were afoot that would lead to Burkinshaw's departure from Tottenham. Paul Bobroff and Irving Scholar engineered a take-over and sold a new tranche of shares to make Tottenham a publicly owned company with a listing on the Stock Exchange, the first such football club to do so. Burkinshaw, unhappy about the proposed changes, also fell out with striker Steve Archibald when he refused to allow the substitution of Archibald in the first home game of the season. Their relationship, never very strong, collapsed with the two protagonists completely ignoring each other. Spurs slipped to 8th in the League in 1983-84 and made early exits from both domestic Cup competitions but in Europe they stormed to the UEFA Cup Final where they would face Anderlecht. Unhappily, following a 1-1 draw in Belgium in the first leg, Steve Perryman was suspended for the home leg and missed out on the celebrations but Spurs won the Cup on penalties following a 1-1 draw, with goalkeeper Tony Parks making the vital save.

As he announced his resignation the next day Keith Burkinshaw, looked at the new West Stand and made the withering observation, "There used to be a football club over there!"

Looking back today, he can see an awful lot of similarity in Spurs' decision to ditch Mauricio Pochettino for Jose Mourinho to the way the club sent him packing expecting Alex Ferguson to replace him. Unfortunately for Spurs Fergie opted for a move to Manchester United instead, leaving Tottenham high and dry. Burkinshaw has every sympathy for Pochettino but the comparison is not complete because while Keith Burkinshaw filled the club's trophy cabinet with silverware Pochettino failed to win a trophy at Spurs.

Burkinshaw rarely relives the ending of his time at Spurs as it brings back too many painful memories, but he spoke to me for this book. "The proudest, most memorable moment was winning our first trophy, the FA Cup. We had some great times with a great team back then, but the club hadn't won anything since Billy Nick's day and winning the FA Cup was a huge achievement, with some great players, playing good football, but a trophy to show for it all, so that would rank as the highlight of all my years as manager of Spurs.

"The saddest… well, leaving the club the way that I did. Regrets, yes, for sure, plenty. It was the saddest moment of my Spurs time, leaving the day after winning the UEFA Cup. I left straight away, it was awful. With the players we had, the players coming through the ranks, I was sure we would push on and have even more success, although of course, nothing is guaranteed in football, so I cannot be absolutely sure.

"The directors and owners thought they had Alex Ferguson wrapped up. There was a lot going on behind my back that you only get to realise after you've left. It was one of those things where the owners thought they knew better than the manager, and to be fair, times haven't changed too much in that respect generally in football.

"For me, one of the most important, if not the single most important aspects of football, should be man-management. Yet, man-management is one of the things most missing in the game, back then, and even now. It should be a big factor in football, man-management of directors and owners, man-management of the coach with their players.

"It was also sad knowing that there were so many talented young players we had been bringing through, and the club let about five or six of them go. Most of them went to Norwich and they reached the quarter finals in Europe a few year on. Those kids had the potential to be really good players at Tottenham, but they didn't keep hold of them."

Burkinshaw's opinion of Mourinho isn't clouded by anything other than his ability to win trophies wherever he has gone. "He is successful, isn't he. Doesn't need much more of an explanation why Spurs went for him. Pochettino was a good coach, well liked by the fans, but he didn't win anything, and the club wanted to start to win trophies again, it's been a long time since the last one."

Keith was the second most successful manager in Tottenham's history after the legendary Nicholson but left for a succession of jobs in the Middle East, including the Bahrain national team, and in Zambia, then Sporting Clube de Portugal before returning to England to manage Gillingham. Burkinshaw was then Chief Scout for Glenn Hoddle and Ossie Ardiles at Swindon Town and in May 1992, he became assistant to Ardiles at West Bromwich Albion. He also had a spell as Director of Football and caretaker manager at Aberdeen, before becoming the assistant manager of Watford, where he helped the club reach the Premier League in 2006.

Lifelong Spurs fan Irving Scholar believed he had already lined up Sir Alex Ferguson to succeed Burkinshaw in May 1984, insisting that he had shaken hands with the Scot, and considered the deal to be done. Scholar said: "The truth was that I had been talking to and negotiating with Alex Ferguson about a deal. He and I had had very long and detailed discussions. I told him that I was a very old-fashioned type of chap and that the most important thing was that once you agree something, once you shake someone's hand, it's in concrete. Once you do that, then you do not — under any circumstances whatsoever — you do not go back on it. It's over. I told him that, when I first met him. So we had this big thing about the handshake."

Scholar, a property tycoon who took control of Tottenham in 1982, knew that Burkinshaw planned to quit at the end of the season because of his dislike to the new business model. Ferguson, though, has his own version of events and claimed that Spurs were not prepared to give him the five-year contract he wanted to burn his bridges at Aberdeen at a time when he was dominating the game up in Scotland, having just secured the League and Cup double. Scholar also believed that when Manchester United came calling a few years later, Ferguson had a bigger incentive to leave Aberdeen.

Burkinshaw was actually replaced by Peter Shreeves who had been elevated through the ranks at Spurs by Burkinshaw, leaving the youth team to take charge of the reserves before he was appointed assistant manager in 1980. He eventually succeeded Burkinshaw and enjoyed two spells as Tottenham boss, leading them to a third-place finish in 1985.

13: PETER SHREEVES

HAVING MANAGED TOTTENHAM FOR THREE years across two different spells, firstly from 1984-86 and then from 1991-92, Peter Shreeves had a wealth of experience in the Spurs hot-seat. The Welshman had been elevated through the ranks at Spurs by Keith Burkinshaw, leaving the youth team to take charge of the reserves before he was appointed assistant manager in 1980. He eventually succeeded Burkinshaw and enjoyed two spells as manager, leading them to a third-place finish in 1985.

Real Madrid were underdogs when they arrived at White Hart Lane for the first leg of their UEFA Cup quarter-final in March 1985. A recent run of just one win in 10 matches had taken them out of the race for La Liga, as Terry Venables Barcelona were walking away with the title and Madrid would go on to finish fifth.

Peter Shreeves could not have asked for a better start to his Tottenham reign after taking over from Keith Burkinshaw. Sitting second in the table behind Everton, the club were aiming to win their first league title since 1961.

In contrast to Real, their run to the last eight of the UEFA Cup had been relatively stress-free; A 9-0 aggregate win over Braga was followed by a 4-2 win against Club Brugge. In the 3-1 victory over Bohemians Prague in the third round, Glenn Hoddle and Graham Roberts left the pitch with stitches during a bruising second leg in Prague, with Roberts also picking up a booking that kept him out of the first leg of the quarter-final at White Hart Lane. Given Real Madrid's home form in the competition, Tottenham were desperate to take a sizeable advantage to the Bernabéu. Real were nothing like the teams of their notable brilliant past, nothing like the force of today. Yet with talent such as José Antonio Camacho, Uli Stielike, Ricardo Gallego, Emilio Butragueño, Santillana and Jorge Valdano, they had enough to threaten Tottenham's proud record of never losing a home match in Europe.

With Paul Miller and Tony Galvin fit, Gary Stevens moved to centre-back to fill in for Roberts and Mickey Hazard returned to the team, confidence was high in the Spurs camp. But a determined Real Madrid team left London with a slender lead. The only goal came after 14 minutes, a crucial away goal. For the first time in 44 ties in European competition, Spurs had failed to score at home.

"It doesn't please me to say that Real played some superb stuff at times," said Shreeves at the time. "This is a night when we must salute the victors. It will need a special performance in the return game if we are to get through." As the crowd of 39,914 filed out of White Hart Lane, the Tottenham PA announcer boldly said: "This tie is far from over."

After their first win at Anfield since 1921, Spurs confidence was high going to Madrid. Mark Falco had a goal disallowed and Steve Perryman was sent off three minutes later as Real progressed 1-0 on aggregate and went on to lift the trophy. Shreeves would never experience such highs again. Five defeats in Tottenham's remaining league fixtures – all suffered at White Hart Lane – left them third in the First Division before Shreeves suffered second-season syndrome and, come May 1986, he was replaced by David Pleat.

Nevertheless, Shreeves' debut season had been impressive. No Spurs manager improved on his third-place finish in 1984-85 until Mauricio Pochettino secured second place in the Premier League in 2016/17. In that first season, Spurs had finished level on points with Liverpool, having been top on New Year's Day after winning at Arsenal and but for a poor run of home form in the second half of the season when Spurs lost 6 out of 8 games and a number of serious injuries, they would have been much closer to champions, Everton.

Throughout the following season, Spurs were constantly in mid-table. It had started well with a 4–0 home win over Watford with new signings Paul Allen and Chris Waddle scoring. That put them as early leaders but it was downhill for the rest of the season. Following a win over West Ham on Boxing Day, Spurs went until late February without a league win, taking one point from six games. Spurs then lost at home to Liverpool and had dropped to 13th in the league.

Amid talk of unrest in the dressing room, it was clear Shreeves would be leaving White Hart Lane in the summer. From early March Spurs results showed a great improvement with only one defeat, at Upton Park, in 12 games. The sequence of results included eight wins with a number of high-scoring victories starting with a 5–0 home win over West Bromwich Albion. They also won 4–1 at Leicester City and finished the season by scoring 14 goals in their final three games – winning 5-2 at Queen's Park Rangers and with 4–2 and 5–3 home wins over Aston Villa and Southampton respectively. The only blemish in Tottenham's record to the end of the 1985-86 season was a 2–1 defeat at Upton Park. In the previous game they had defeated Arsenal at the Lane, but at Upton Park West Ham took a first half lead. Ossie Ardiles equalised within five minutes but West Ham regained the lead two minutes before the interval. Although Clive Allen hit the post in the second half after replacing Ardiles, Spurs suffered their first defeat in five games. Tottenham finished 10th and the late run of results came too late to save Shreeves.

He started life as a taxi driver, and now it was time to call "taxi for Peter Shreeves" and to be replaced by David Pleat.

Yet Peter remains well liked by many Spurs players he managed as well as held in high esteem by Spurs fans. I always enjoyed his company, and felt that his best role was "looking after" Keith Burkinshaw. He often needed to be his minder, his punch bag with the players if the manager was being too strict or aloof. There was never a dull moment in those days, as you would often be privy to some of the more bizarre goings on.

A flight back from one of Spurs' European adventures provided one such bizarre episodes, watching a furtive Shreeves following Keith Burkinshaw as he paced up and down at the check in desk looking very grim. I was part of a small contingent of senior football writers who accompanied teams like Spurs on their big European excursions. Keith was the far more serious type, but his assistant Peter Shreeves had a much more affable sociable streak to his nature, a contrast to the dour Yorkshireman. At this time, the media would travel with the team, with the club lightning the financial burden of the trips with the newspapers, TV and radio footing part of the bill. So on the morning of our return flight , it was not a surprise to see the managerial pair together, as they would invariably be side by side, but on this occasion it soon became apparent that all was not well by the body language of the manger and that of his assistant. Both were extremely agitated to say the least.

The conversation between the two went on for some considerable time, and got more heated by the minute. We were all wondering what was going on. Then it quickly became apparent the cause of the problem. Enter England goalkeeper Ray Clemence being supported by Spurs staff dragging him along towards the departure lounge. One of the country's most respected players had a very stupid grin on his face, and he was bellowing out a song at the top of his voice that made sure it was impossible not to notice his entrance. It should be pointed out at this juncture, that he was no Harry Redknapp or Sam Allarydce, and he couldn't sing!

But Ray did not stop signing at the top of his voice, all the way up the stairs of the plane, as he was helped to his seat. Once seated he instantly feel asleep, and we were left in blissful silence. As he drifted off into a very deep sleep all was very peaceful again, except for Burkinshaw's mood; the manager was fuming, and it was easy to see why. Clemence had been out the night before and had got back to his hotel bedroom after all the Spurs party had left the hotel for the airport. Clearly, therefore, no one saw him returning. Worse still, no one missed him. Oblivious at the time to the entire Spurs staff and the players, he went off to sleep in his room and was still in his bed fast asleep when a couple of the Spurs staff were assigned to return to the hotel to find him, while the charter flight was held up.

Peter asked the small group of journalists who were travelling with the team not to report this incident. We all agreed. It was a vastly different era in the early 80s. For a start, these days the media party no longer travel with a team or stay in the same hotel, unless it cannot be avoided. The barriers between press and players have risen over the years, keeping pace with the way the media has mushroomed. Now there can be five or six representatives form one newspaper if a game is big enough and warrants blanket coverage, and even in routine games with the big clubs there might well be two reporters and a news man present. Whereas back then there would be just the one to file a match report and perhaps a bit of transfer gossip, so it was far easier for clubs that to control the output, particularly if things went wrong as they did on that day with Spurs. The press pack would often go out drinking with the players, I've even been to a nightclub with a group of players with a London club after a European tie abroad, and no one worried about anything being reported in the press, we would keep their minor indiscretions to ourselves if we were invited into their inner sanctum.

Hence no one ever read bout Ray's boozy flight home – until now of course!

14: GERRY FRANCIS

GERRY FRANCIS ONCE INVITED ME TO THE Playboy Club in central London. It was his meeting place of choice for his contribution to my first ever book, 'The Treatment of Football Injuries' in conjunction with the then Spurs physiotherapist Mike Varney. Gerry was England captain at the time and one of the most famous footballers of his generation but he was also one of the first to try alternative medicines and manipulation techniques for a persistent back complaint, so he was able to give me a unique insight into how those techniques had helped a top class footballer, in the kind of surroundings that might raise some eyebrows and banner headlines nowadays!

I got to know Gerry much better when he became manager of Spurs, one of Alan Sugar's appointments. Francis kept a diary during one of the most turbulent times in the club's history. He would file weekly entries, gave them to others to scan through and then forgot about them. "When I got them back, I couldn't put them down," he says. "And I wrote it!" Those dairies formed the basis of a book 'The Team That Dared To Do', the story of the season Tottenham finished seventh

It tells how Spurs have always been ambitious, have always had style, however when he joined in 1994-95 Francis lured us away from chaos following the chaos of Ossie Ardiles' reign and took us to seventh place in the Premier League, making Tottenham the best London club that season. Francis had been appointed mid-season and within 27 minutes of his opening match Spurs were 3-0 down!

His predecessor, the much loved Ossie Ardiles, had constructed a side around the "famous five" of Jürgen Klinsmann, Teddy Sheringham, Ilie Dumitrescu, Darren Anderton and Nick Barmby, with goals flowing at both ends. Spurs lost eight of their opening 16 matches, scoring 29 but conceding 35. In Ossie's penultimate game Spurs were knocked out of the League Cup 3-0 away to

Notts County.

Francis had to resolve the style of play but he also had to contend with all the off the field politics that had engulfed the club. Francis recalled: "They'd had 12 points deducted, reduced to six on appeal, and been banned from the FA Cup." It all pointed to a recipe for relegation. Francis continued: "They were doing so poorly. I had no money — didn't spend a penny that year — and so I had exactly the same players. Improvement would come from within."

Francis had been a mainstay for Queens Park Rangers during the 1970s and captained England during his time at Loftus Road but he grew up supporting Spurs during the glory, glory days, 1961-62.

When Alan Sugar, approached him about the top job at Spurs, Francis was at a crossroads. "I was really pissed off with football. When I met Alan he talked about me being a coach and working with a Director of Football. I just said, 'No, I'm not interested,' and went home. I could have called it a day.

"It was what they had done to me at QPR, trying to get rid of me because they wanted to sell Les Ferdinand and I wouldn't. I had already sold players and got them into the top five. It's impossible to do, really. Alan said there wasn't any money — it's not like Tottenham now — but I had spent all my career at clubs with no money."

Francis took up the challenge and he was in charge at the club for three years at the start of the Premier League era. In his first diary entry he speaks of the stature of Spurs, "Until you work here, you don't realise just how big it is and how much tradition is attached to the place," he wrote. "It is massive. You see people like Bill Nicholson around and you know you are somewhere special."

Spurs lost 4-3 to Aston Villa in his first game, but his first 16 fixtures brought drastic change — 32 points, only two defeats, seven clean sheets. Eventually the points deduction and cup suspension were overturned and Spurs reached the FA Cup semi-final, and Jürgen Klinsmann scored 30 goals in all competitions.

At QPR Francis had been interviewed about the England job

and another interview would follow when he was doing so well at Spurs, however Francis said: "I was so happy at Spurs. No other Premier League manager has turned two teams into the top club in London. I'm proud of my record."

Francis would later return to QPR, and to Bristol Rovers, but a series of family bereavements made him "completely stop football". But he returned to work alongside Tony Pulis at Stoke City, Crystal Palace and West Bromwich Albion.

Francis still admires the "magical club" and the work Mauricio Pochettino. Commenting prior to the Argentine coach's sacking Francis said: "He has put together a very good team, but what he needs now is trophies. You can have two or three fantastic years, then have a sticky spell and the pressure is on, because people panic in the Premier League now. They are capable of challenging for things."

When Jose Mourinho replaced Pochettino, Francis suggested that Spurs supporters need to acknowledge trophies aren't always won with free-flowing football. Mourinho would deliver trophies, but the fans had to compromise their devotion to the glory, glory game and accept their new manager's methods; it was a question of style or substance? "I can see why the club's chairman Daniel Levy wanted to get Mourinho, because everything else is in place; the stadium and the team," says Francis, "what you haven't got is trophies. And whatever people say about Mourinho, he does bring trophies. Jose has won more trophies in his career than Tottenham have won in their whole history." Gerry is correct; Mourinho has laid claim to 20 pieces of major silverware, including three League titles in England and four European cup competitions. Spurs have just 17 major trophies since they were formed in 1882, two league titles and three European triumphs.

In an interview in the Sunday Express, Francis was convinced the club was hampered by the tradition of playing with flair, something the Spurs fans still take so much pride in, but it can overshadow the quest for success in real terms. "There is no doubt in my mind, having managed the club for three years, and having watched Tottenham all the way through from the 1960s to the present day, it is a difficult club. That's because the fans like to see you winning but they also want you to win with style. And that's not always possible. Obviously, it's completely different to my days at Tottenham. They have progressed to being always in the top four in the last few years and reaching the Champions League final. They moved up under Mauricio Pochettino, but you still look at it and say, 'What's he won?'

"Getting to the Champions League final was a magnificent achievement, but do people remember second places? Pochettino's team has been excellent, with the pressing football he brought from Southampton and the flair his team played with. I enjoyed watching them, they played great stuff and you always felt that on their day they could beat anyone. He did so well in so many ways. Off the field the club has grown fantastically to have the best stadium and the best training facilities in the country if not the whole of Europe. But he was there more than five years – and what was won? Mauricio really needed to win a trophy, whether it was the League Cup or the FA Cup. It helps all round with a club if you can win trophies – certainly with the players who become even more hungry to win silverware. Because that's really what it's all about, winning silverware. That defines your period at a club in football history."

Francis believed it was a risk worth taking for the club to land some elusive silverware. "The pattern has been for Jose to win trophies in the first or second season, and then for complications and problems to arise. That happened at Real Madrid, Chelsea and Manchester United. He comes with some baggage, but also a glittering array of trophies. The question to be answered now, for me, is can Daniel Levy and Jose have a relationship that works? And will the fans accept Mourinho trying to win things with Tottenham using a methodical style of football.

"Jose has a tremendous record, he is a serial winner, and it's built on getting a lead and then closing a match out. That's exactly what Spurs haven't done in recent times; they've been 2-0 up and not won the match, and they have kept losing leads. He will get Spurs organised, he plays the way he plays; you could call it winning football, I suppose. To win titles you need to be a consistent side winning matches all through the season. Will winning titles or cups make up for not playing with much flair week in, week out? I am certain that Tottenham fans want to win things, but they also love the club's tradition of playing with style."

Going back to Gerry's spell in the White Hart Lane hot-seat, in the eyes of many Spurs fans Alan Sugar's reign as chairman between 1995 to 2001 was an unmitigated disaster, and they would happily hold up those cards in union to say "You're Fired!" However, in Sugars' defence, he knew precious little about the intricacies of football, precious less about who best to appoint as manager. And why should he?   Owners pitch up with so limited knowledge, they invariably have to rely on advice. It's a question of who gives the advice, and whether you take it or not.

For many Spurs fans of this period, they would not look back on Gerry Francis period in charge with much affection, accusing him of being too defensive minded. While star names such as Klinsmann, Popescu, Barmby, Sheringham and Dumitrescu were sold, and in came the likes of Armstrong, Fox, Sinton, Scales, Vega, Iversen, Dominguez and Neilsen, although to be fair he did bring in Les Ferdinand and David Ginola.

But there was a long list of some of the games greats that Spurs missed out on at the time such as Dennis Bergkamp, Juninho, Eyal Berkovic and Ruud Gullit, while Emmanuel Petit pitched up at Spurs but then famously caught a taxi to Highbury to sign for them! I can certainly tell you from first hand experience that Dennis Bergkamp wanted to sign for Spurs, and should have been a Spurs star instead of one of Arsenal's greatest ever players, but that Francis wasn't interested, because he 'didn't score enough goals"!

A very close friend of mine at the time, a prominent journalist in Holland, rang me to say that Dennis wanted to quit Italy where he had not been enjoying his football with Inter Milan because of the negative attitude of the league at that time. Bergkamp had not scored a single goal in open play all season, having netted just once from the penalty spot. The journalist told me Dennis wanted to try his luck in England, had always been a Spurs fan because of his boyhood hero worship of Glenn Hoddle, whose picture he had on his bedroom wall as a kid, and asked if Spurs interested?

I rang Alan Sugar. He was still plain Alan Sugar back then. Would the Spurs chairman like the opportunity to sign Dennis Bergkamp? "Dennis who?" replied Alan.

"Dennis Bergkamp. He's a fantastic footballer, can score goals, make them, brilliant signing for Spurs and reasonably priced, something like £3 million is all that it might take, no higher than £5 million taking into account all the add ons and agents fees."

I can hear Alan Sugar shouting for his son Daniel's attention. "Who's Dennis Bergkamp?" there was a pause and a muffled conversation before Alan comes back on and says, "Oh, ok then…". He said he would make some enquiries with his manager, Gerry Francis, and come back to me the next day. I didn't hear anything the next day, so I called him back the day after, thinking that the club have probably made some enquiries of their own. Wrong, they hadn't!

Alan told me that he was very thankful for my help, but that I should tell whoever I was talking to that Spurs were not interested. Gerry Francis didn't fancy him, Alan explained, as the manager wanted an out-and-out goalscoring striker and he felt that Bergkamp was more of a midfielder and he had plenty of them. Gerry went on to sign striker Chris Armstrong from Crystal Palace instead. Arsenal fan and sports lawyer Mel Goldberg, who specialised in transfers, had been a very close friend of mine over the years. He then offered Dennis Bergkamp to Arsenal and was shocked how the price suddenly went up to £7.5 million but that's another story, for another day, and another book! Of course, we all know now that it didn't take long for the Dutchman to make his mark in English football at Highbury.

15: SPURS WORST MANAGERS

WHEN IT COMES TO CANDIDATES FOR THE worst Spurs manager of all time, there is quite a long list, so please bear with me as this may take some time! The candidates here are not necessarily based purely on whether the managers brought silverware to the club, as two of them actually managed to win the League Cup, but whether they connected with the fans and generally improved the standing of Tottenham. All of them failed that test for one reason or another, in my humble opinion.

In November 1997 CHRISTIAN GROSS arrived from Swiss outfit Grasshopper Club Zürich following the departure of Gerry Francis, clutching a London underground ticket from Heathrow airport to Seven Sisters tube station. He arrived late for his first Spurs press conference and sat down alongside chairman Alan Sugar brandishing his Underground ticket and claiming in limited English that "I want this to become my ticket to the dreams" but Gross was dealt a blow when his most trusted aide, the Swiss fitness coach Fritz Schmid, who had been an integral part of Gross's training plans at Grasshopper, was denied a work permit to take up his planned role at White Hart Lane.

On November 27th 1997, Gross took charge of Tottenham for the first time. Crystal Palace were the visitors to White Hart Lane but a 1-0 defeat in front of 26,634 supporters got him off to the worst possible start. An away win at Everton followed with goals from Ramon Vega and David Ginola, followed by a 6-1 hammering at home to Chelsea, then a 4-0 defeat at Coventry City.

I told Alan Sugar at the time that Gross would have a tough time convincing the media and the fans of his credentials as no one had heard of him and it seemed a huge risk. Alan assured me at the time that Gross had come highly recommended, and that his thinking was to go for a coach with a good reputation rather than

Christian Gross's bizarre press unveiling.
It was all downhill from there to be honest...

a 'big name' who might not even have any real coaching skills and lived off his reputation. Presumably Alan was thinking of the impact Arsene Wenger had enjoyed up the road but I wasn't convinced.

Before he appointed Gross I rang Alan to let him know that a good contact of mine involved with Swedish football said that Sven-Goran Eriksson was interested in the vacant Spurs job. At that time Eriksson had a fantastic reputation on the continent as one of the best coaches and would have been a huge catch having been a success in Sweden, Portugal and Italy

Of course in his later years, starting from the second half of his stint as England boss and his subsequent fall from grace, perhaps not, but at the time Eriksson was the perfect fit for Spurs and would have in all probability done a fantastic job as he had done in his travels around Europe where he had won the league in Portugal three times with Benfica and had just won Serie A with Lazio. When I rang Alan he hadn't heard of Eriksson, which was not a huge surprise, but he said he would consult with a few people and get back to me. We talked again the next day and Sugar said he was not for Spurs. Gross, though, came highly recommended by Jurgen Klinsmann's agent, and that seemed to be good enough for the Spurs chairman!

Gross led Spurs to the brink of relegation in his first season and only the return of Jurgen Klinsmann saved the club from the drop. His nine-month spell came to an end three games into the 1998-99 season. Although Sugar blamed the media, his results left the fans fearing the worst. Nine wins from 27 games give him every right to be dubbed one of the worst Spurs managers of all time and Alan Sugar didn't thank me for telling him "I told you so".

While Ossie Ardiles' points per game average was lower than that of Gross (1.15 v. 1.31) Spurs fans adored Ossie and what he tried to do with his 'Famous Five' forward line, whereas supporters were more than willing to have a whip round for Gross's return Underground ticket well before Sugar uttered his immortal catchphrase "You're fired!"

Sidney Wale was an 'old school' style of football chairman. He never gave interviews and was rarely even pictured, let alone made public appearances or statements. However, as the local *Weekly Herald* sports editor I had grown to know Sidney for long enough for him to trust me, so when I approached him in an empty White Hart Lane car park in the week that he and his Board had appointed Bill Nicholson's successor, I didn't miss my opportunity to ask him why he had chosen ex-Arsenal man TERRY NEILL to be the next Spurs boss in succession to one of English football's greatest ever managers?

"Did he play for Arsenal?" came Sidney's bewildered and shocked response!

Did he play for Arsenal, indeed! Good grief! You would think the men appointing such an important employee would know his CV! Or perhaps not. At that time directors such as Sydney would have read the *Financial Times* or *The Times* and rarely bothered with the back pages.

I spoke with Bill about the appointment of his successor and he thought that, after a lifetime at the club and all that he had achieved for the club, and all the sacrifices he made for Spurs, the Board would have consulted him as they had said they would when asking him to carry on until they found a replacement.

In fact Bill felt he had been badly let down and had wasted his time trying to help the board with soundings to Johnny Giles and his willingness to take the job. Still, there wasn't a dull day with Terry Neill around. Although to be fair he wasn't around for long.

One sunny afternoon and for a reason that I can now no longer accurately recall, there was a challenge thrown down and Terry and I found ourselves racing around the dirt track surrounding the famous White Hart Lane pitch. I think I might have made some reference to Terry looking fit and trim, and he properly made a derogatory remark towards me as usual, perhaps suggesting that I was nowhere near as fit as he was and the ensuing foot race was the result! A bet was laid and off we set. I took the first bend well ahead, I was always good in a sprint, but that spurred Terry to kick on and he ended up the winner by some distance as it was far too much for me over such a distance. As you can see by the photo overleaf, I'm miles behind!

That race seemed to sum up; Terry was never going to conform to the managerial norm, but my relationship with him continued when he became Arsenal manager and long after his managerial career came to an end when he opened a wine bar and restaurant close to the Mirror building in Holborn. That meant I actually saw much more of Terry in "Terry Neill's" then I had when he was in the game! After a good few years with the Mirror hacks like myself keeping him in business, he sold the wine bar and headed back to Ireland.

While Neill was never appreciated or loved in one sector of north London, he was adored by Gunners. Neill spent two years at White Hart Lane before taking over at Arsenal from Bertie Mee at the age of 34 (the club's youngest Arsenal manager to date). An outstanding centre-back at Arsenal, he eventually became the club's manager between 1976 and 1983. During his seven year reign at

Your author trails Tottenham boss Terry Neill by a few lengths coming into the home straight.

Arsenal he guided them to a trio of F.A. Cup finals (1978, 1979 and 1980) but only won in 1979. He reached the Cup Winners' Cup final in 1980 losing to Valencia on penalties, Graham Rix and Liam Brady both missing from the spot, before he was sacked in 1983 after a League Cup exit to Walsall.

GEORGE GRAHAM enjoyed nine largely golden years with Arsenal, winning the title twice in three seasons and doing more than any other club to break Liverpool's stranglehold on English football, before he was appointed Spurs manager in October 1998. Arsenal had just completed their first double since 1971 three months previously under Arsene Wenger playing a very different style of football from that under Graham and, following a one-year ban following his sacking by Arsenal for accepting a 'bung', Graham had spent two years reviving the fortunes of Leeds United but for many Tottenham fans the Arsenal link was too much to stomach, and they never warmed to the manager or his pragmatic style of play.

Once again I told Alan Sugar that it was a strange decision to go for Graham, so intrinsically linked to Arsenal, and one of their greatest legends as both player and manager. I agreed with Sugar that he was appointing a man with a great reputation as a manager with an impressive CV, but I also told him that Graham would never be taken into the hearts of Spurs fans and that it would "all end in tears". Sugar would get aggressive if you contradicted him, but he knew I was making the point for his best interests and in the best interests of Spurs, and to a degree he confessed that he shared some of my reservations, but he explained how he had left it to what he considered to be the 'professional' element he had recruited to his Board to make these sort of tough decisions that invariably chairman are not qualified to make, and the overwhelming view had been to go for Graham.

While his appointment went down like a lead balloon as you would expect, he at least won the League Cup in 1999 in his first season, Alan Sugar's only piece of silverware in his entire reign at the Lane. That was Graham's seventh trophy as a manager – following two championships, two League Cups, an FA Cup and a Cup-Winners' Cup with Arsenal, he was second only to Sir Alex Ferguson among working managers at that time.

Yet Graham was sacked in March 2001 hot on the heels of the club's poor financial results, the first since investment group ENIC took a stake. The new owners sacked Graham for a breach of confidentiality by talking to journalists about the club's financial position. After three years in charge he departed within a month of Daniel Levy taking over from Sugar.

Graham had met with Tottenham executive vice-chairman David Buchler, who arrived with ENIC, to discuss future strategy. When asked about his future at Spurs Graham gave an honest answer, "I had a long meeting with the vice-chairman this week and gave him my recommendations. I have been told there is a limited budget. But my own contract situation never arose, and it is not up until the end of next season." That public statement about what Buchler considered to be a private internal meeting proved to be Graham's downfall.

Despite reaching the semi-finals of the FA Cup, where Spurs were due to confront Arsenal, the recent run of poor football performance damaged Graham's reputation. "Results on the pitch have not been satisfactory for many years," Spurs' new chairman Daniel Levy said in a statement after Graham was sacked. Buchler added that Graham had already received written warnings for similar offences and that he had been summarily dismissed for breaking his contract. "I don't think that that's a way to run the affairs of this club," Buchler added, "in fact I think it is an appalling way to run this club."

Ever since taking control ENIC had been keen to make changes at White Hart Lane. Levy said that a strategic review of the club's operations had been implemented. "We agreed we cannot work with each other," Buchler said of Graham, "I am not prepared to have someone who is not a team player and who is not looking after the club's interests." Levy had taken the reigns from Sir Alan Sugar as chairman following ENIC's purchase of a 27% stake in the club. "On completion of the strategic review later in the year, I will be in a much better position to communicate our view of the future," said Levy.

Tottenham faced the possibility of losing three key players at the time of the transition from Sugar to ENIC; Sol Campbell, Darren Anderton and Les Ferdinand, under freedom of contract and Buchler questioned the timing of Graham's revelations, on the day he was holding talks with Campbell's agent. "I question the whole timing of it because this is a very delicate and important time for the club," he said.

George Graham - my part in his downfall!

Here I must confess that I played a part in Graham's dismissal! I noticed Graham on the ITV local news programme 'London Tonight' complaining about his player transfer budget, the fact that he couldn't spend as much as he had wanted. This was a sore point with Sugar, who was often criticised by the Spurs fans for not spending enough, when in reality, during his reign the club was among the biggest spenders in the country. I knew Graham's abrasive remarks would hit a raw nerve with Sugar and so pursued the matter in the interests of obtaining a good story for the *Mirror* by tracking down David Buchler, the club's executive vice-chairman, for a reaction. I got one. It proved to be a pretty powerful one at that, and was clearly the prelude to a confrontation between George and the Board that led to Graham's departure.

Buchler might never have responded publicly if I hadn't been successful in tracking him down, as an article in the *Sunday Telegraph* at the time reported in graphic detail. Colin Malam's analysis of how Graham came to be sacked included a section devoted to my involvement in the affair, as he wrote, "The strangest thing about the whole affair is the rather implausible explanation

Buchler gave for the appearance in the *Mirror* on Friday, the day every other newspaper eagerly carried Graham's complaint about a 'limited budget', of an exclusive story quoting the Executive Vice-Chairman as telling the manager to shut up. According to Buchler, it came about quite by chance. 'It so happened that when I came out of a meeting on Thursday night at about 6pm,' he said, 'I put my phone on to ring my wife. I pressed the green button and, instead of getting my wife, Harry Harris, the *Mirror*'s chief football writer, had just phoned in. He asked me if I knew about Graham's remarks. I said "no" and added that it was not the sort of thing I wanted to have discussed in the press. I really didn't think that the press should know about the intricacies of a meeting.'"

The fact that Buchler thought it all happened "quite by chance" was not entirely accurate. It was down to my persistence, not chance, and I tried to get hold of him a hundred times, if not more, until contact was made! I was determined to get hold of him as I knew the fragile position of Graham at this time, and knew that this might easily push him over the edge. Colin Malam pointed out that to publicly express concern about having a limited transfer budget is an old tried and tested managerial ploy to prise more cash out of the Board, but not at Tottenham, and not at that time. Graham must have known the score, must have known he was taking a huge risk with his outspoken criticism, it was as if he was pressing the self-destruct button. So just three weeks before the 2001 FA Cup semi-final against Arsenal, Graham was sacked when Buchler called him in the next day for an explanation of his comments.

Did I play a part in Graham's demise? Colin Malam seemed to think so, and I am not going to argue with such an esteemed football writer of the time.

Spanish coach JUANDE RAMOS looked back on his first days as Spurs manager back in 2008 in a fascinating article in *The Guardian* which provided a shocking insight into the way the club had been run. When he and his staff walked into the dining room at the training ground they thought of asking "where was the wedding?"

"'Incredible,' Ramos said, shaking his head, 'it was like a wedding buffet; cakes, pastries, sauces – and that was what they ate regularly. Honestly, and I say this with no bitterness at all, there were players who were, well, fat.'

"He laughs: 'They were sedentary.'

"He elaborated: 'A sportsman's physical condition has to be impeccable: your body is your living. A runner is like this. You can't live like the man on the street who's had dessert or cake. If you eat a cake, you're putting in diesel; a sportsman's got to run off super. A sportsman who makes, say, £6m and drinks and smokes and eats, it makes no sense at all. A lad who's 22, 23 and has cash might think: "This guy's not telling me what to eat." We train not far from a McDonald's and we'd see them in there eating hamburgers, drinking Coke but you explain and they understand. "This is your ideal weight, the percentage of body fat." I can't go to their houses to watch them eating but we could train morning and afternoon and weigh them. If you're not in shape, you don't play and with work the team started improving.'"

Under Ramos Spurs won their last trophy, the 2008 Carling Cup having beaten Arsenal in the semi-finals and Chelsea in the final. It was the club's first trophy for nine years and only their second in 17 years. Yet Ramos was sacked with the team bottom of the table with two points from their opening eight games at the start of the following season. He was dismissed one day short of a year after taking charge following a 2-1 defeat by Stoke in October 2008 which left Spurs rooted to the bottom of the Premier League with just 2 points from 8 games.

At Sevilla he won five trophies but he was never given any credence or recognition as a manager in the Premier League. However he insisted that, "At White Hart Lane they'll have good memories: the last title that Spurs won was with me, so I guess they'll remember me fondly." Unfortunately, they probably can't remember him much at all!

"We hadn't beaten Arsenal for years and we won 5-1. We won the Carling Cup, everyone's really happy... " And then? "I was sacked. Levy had an easy explanation: 'No, the thing is, the coach doesn't get it, the players are hungry, they don't eat, he doesn't understand ...' When we won the Carling Cup I understood and then I don't understand any more! They sacked a manager they'd given a four-year contract to. So they say: 'He didn't understand!'"

He counters the view held at the time that he had little or no relationship with the players. "My relationship with them was excellent," Ramos said, "you know who it was bad with? [David] Bentley."

He has a bit more to complain about: "The year before they'd signed Darren Bent for £17m. They sell Robbie Keane and Berbatov because they want Bent to play, so they left us with Darren Bent and Frazier Campbell. Without strikers!" And Roman Pavlyuchenko? "Yes but he was new to England, didn't understand and hardly played – and not just under me. I'm sure that if Levy had known what would happen he would have either not sold Berbatov or signed a replacement. But he wanted Bent to play and Bent had a brilliant pre-season, so Levy thinks: 'We've got the players. Bent scored 12 or 13 during pre-season. That's the worst thing that could happen!' So Levy says: 'This guy [Berbatov] out, this guy [Keane] out... Berbatov didn't want to stay. Against Middlesbrough he said: 'No, no, I'm not playing.' I understood. It's more honourable to say 'I don't want to play' than to go out and not even try. If he stays and he's pissed off, he's pissed off all year. In my opinion, the problem isn't selling him and Keane, it's not replacing them.

"I wanted Samuel Eto'o and David Villa. Eto'o wanted too much in wages. We negotiated with Villa, when he was one of the world's best. Levy's a hard negotiator and in the end it didn't happen. So we were left with Bent and Campbell. We couldn't beat anyone. We couldn't have scored if we'd used a rainbow as the goalposts."

Yours truly and Spurs last piece of silverware

Ramos could see that Gareth Bale was going to be very good but the Welshman spent eight months injured. He also speaks highly of Jermaine Jenas who "always offered tactical solutions", describes Tom Huddlestone as like "a bear" with a "scandalously good touch" and calls Jonathan Woodgate a "very good, intelligent player". But Woodgate, as with Ledley King, was injury prone and Michael Dawson was "still just a kid". He remembers: "We could only use King in important games: he didn't train, which was a pity. He was so talented. Even at 50%, he was the leader but, sadly, you can't fight for the titles like that. So, eight weeks into the season – I'm out! Then what happens? In December they spent £51m to rectify the mistake. Defoe, Keane, Kaboul, Palacios. £51m! 'No, the manager doesn't understand... it's the coach, that silly little Spaniard who hasn't got a clue... I took the blame but they had to spend £51m to sort it out. The honourable thing Levy did was sack [director of football Damien] Comolli too: if he'd truly blamed the signings on me, Comolli would have continued but the whole structure changed. He knew but when it came to the [message to] the press and fans, it was the manager's fault. They know they ruined the team when they sold two strikers and left me none."

The Spaniard admits he also made mistakes. "Of course. I shouldn't have accepted some decisions that weren't mine. I can't think of a specific thing I'd change but the responsibility for the team is mine, absolutely. I accepted Comolli's players, who I hadn't proposed. That was a mistake." Perhaps he should have refused to work with Comolli? "With hindsight that might have been the right thing to do."

Ramos added: "Spurs works as a business. That's legitimate and I'm sure the model's built with the right intentions. They think the economic model enables the sporting model to function but that's not always true. Levy makes a £17m investment [Bent] but has two better players in the way. They have to remove obstacles so the investment plays. In economic terms, fine. In sporting terms it turned out to be a disaster.

"Spurs spend a lot of money but only sign players who are 20 or 22 because they're thinking of future sales. Bale, for example, or Modric: I advised Spurs to sign him. He's a great player but you still need patience; it doesn't happen immediately. The idea is: sign players, see if they take off, sell and reinvest. Fine but are you trying to win money or titles? The criteria at Manchester United, Manchester City, Chelsea is that the sporting side is the priority. If City sign Navas or Negredo, they don't look at the player's age; they look at his performances.

"Spurs aren't going to win the league. Economically, it works well but in sporting terms maybe it needs retuning. You can't demand something that doesn't fit the reality."

THE LAST PIECE OF SILVERWARE

Tottenham 2 Chelsea 1 (at Wembley) (aet)

Juande Ramos restored goalkeeper Paul Robinson to the team alongside new signings Alan Hutton and Jonathan Woodgate, replacing the injured Michael Dawson, made their first appearances in the competition. Tottenham surprised Chelsea as they took the game to them, but their London rivals Chelsea came more into the game and Didier Drogba gave Chelsea an undeserved lead late in the first half. On 70 minutes Spurs were awarded a penalty for a handling offence and Dimitar Berbatov remained calm to score the equaliser. In the fourth minute of extra-time Woodgate scored with a header from Jenas' free-kick. Tottenham held out against a final onslaught to win their first trophy in nine years.

Team: Robinson; Hutton, King, Woodgate, Chimbonda (Huddlestone); Lennon, Jenas, Zakora, Malbranque (Tainio); Berbatov, Keane (Kaboul) Subs: (unused): Cerny, Bent.

16: DANIEL LEVY

GARY NEVILLE BELIEVES THE RELATIONSHIP between Jose Mourinho and chairman Daniel Levy is "a marriage of convenience". The decision to appoint Mourinho was an uncharacteristic call by Levy's standards, according to the Sky Sports pundit, whose views are notoriously controversial and generate so much media reaction. For Neville it was a simple equation; Mourinho's desire to return to the Premier League and the chairman's urgent need to keep players like Harry Kane. "If you'd said Levy would hire a manager of Mourinho's stature, that would stand up to him, I would have said not in a million years. For me this is absolutely a bridge for Levy and Mourinho. Mourinho needed to be back in the Premier League and establish himself. He wanted to be back in London. This is a marriage of convenience. Levy is not stupid enough to expose himself to a £25m hit if achievements are not made. They are using each other. It's a hard, cold conversation between two men. Jose wants to be back at the elite level winning trophy, and Levy needs to keep the players he's got. The contract will be that detailed around what he has to do, and ultimately both of them would have protected themselves."

While much has been written about Mourinho, in fact I've written four books about him myself, there is still an enigma about Levy whether is a hero or a villain. To those who believe the priority is to put the best players into the team and to achieve the best possible results, there remains a question mark. Yet for those who believe you need to protect the financial safety of the club, then he is an expert. So he has become the Marmite Man of the Boardroom. If you love him or hate him, it all depends on your view of what the aims of Tottenham Hotspur Football Club should be.

For the man who presided over a near £1billion super stadium, rated one of the best in the world, yet still kept the club's finances under control and oversaw a team that reached the Champions League Final under Mauricio Pochettino and another top four finish, he will be regarded as a mastermind.

To others he is a penny pinching, hard nosed businessman who sometimes over plays his hand in the transfer market in pursuit of a good deal, to the detriment of his manager's desire for the standard of player required to take the team forward.

Levy is "far worse than Manchester United executive vice-chairman Ed Woodward when it comes to signing players," claimed former Chelsea midfielder Craig Burley, now a TV pundit, reacting to the sacking of Pochettino and the hiring of Jose Mourinho. Mourinho fell out with Woodward during his final summer at United after the club failed to bring in the players he wanted in the transfer window. Burley believed Mourinho would face far bigger obstacles from Levy.

At the time of Mourinho's appointment less than five weeks before Christmas, he said on ESPN FC, "Eighteen months ago when he was in the US, Jose Mourinho with United for the ICC pre-season tournament, he was walking around like somebody had told him he'd got two weeks to live. He was miserable because Ed Woodward wasn't giving him what he wanted - well Daniel Levy is Ed Woodward times ten!"

Levy might be the longest serving chairman in the Premier League, yet precious little is known about someone who rarely gives interviews and shuns publicity. He borders on being a recluse by comparison to some high profile chairman! Levy has now sacked ten managers at Spurs, and as Mourinho's career has played out, it seems inevitable that at some stage he will be sacking No. 11!

Levy was born in Essex. His father Barry Levy was the owner of a clothing retail business Mr Byrite (later re-branded as Blue Inc). The company was founded by Abraham Levy and began trading as A. Levy & Sons. They had a hat shop in Stratford, east London. The company traded via a number of brands, chiefly as Mr Byrite, a chain of discount stores selling menswear. The company expanded rapidly in the 1980s and was then run by the three children of Barrie Levy – Jonathan, Robert and Daniel.

Daniel studied Economics and Land Economy at Sidney Sussex College, Cambridge, and graduated in 1985 with a First Class Honours Degree. He was appointed to the Spurs Board in December 2000 and is currently the longest serving Chairman of any Premier League club. He is also Managing Director of the ENIC Group of companies, a sports, entertainment and media group, a position he has held since 1995.

A lifelong Spurs supporter, he attended his first match at the Lane against QPR in the 1960s but when I first met Levy over a convivial dinner near his ENIC offices in the late 1990s, he confessed that he wasn't one of those all consuming passionate regulars. The totally committed Spurs fan in his office was his then secretary Tracy, who later became his wife, who also attended that dinner along with my colleague and good friend, one of the Radio 5Live commentator Alan Green.

Alan and I were pitching to Daniel as a potential investor in our embryonic web site called "Voice of Football", which must have been one of the first on line dedicated football outlets, and with Alan's powerful opinions, my breaking stories reputation on the *Daily Mirror*, and others contributing such as the Chelsea supporting MP and member of the FA's World Cup committee Tony Banks, we had growing interest in our enterprise, including 60s pop pin up turned entrepreneur Adam Faith.

It was over dinner that I suggested to Daniel that he should buy Spurs from Alan Sugar, who was a willing seller at that time. He wasn't convinced but you could tell that his secretary thought it was a smashing idea. Daniel went off to ponder the idea, and not long after that meeting, he contacted me and I put him in touch with Alan Sugar. Levy made an attempt to buy from Sugar in July 1998 but failed. However, Levy was appointed to the board on 20 December 2000 after ENIC initiated the purchase of a 29.8% stake in the club from Sugar for £22 million. He replaced Sugar as chairman in February 2001 on completion of the sale.

Levy was also a director of Glasgow Rangers, in which ENIC

held a significant stake until 2004. In November 2017, Levy was named CEO of the Year at the Football Business Awards. Much has been made of the club's massive financial commitment to the new stadium being responsible for seemingly capped players salaries, and conservatism in the transfer market. So, back in the summer of 2018 the *Evening Standard* conducted a question and answer with Donna Maria-Cullen, perceived as Levy's 'right hand women' on the board.

London Evening Standard: Are Spurs being restricted in the transfer market because of the club's move into their brand new stadium?

Donna Maria-Cullen: "No, no. That is a misconception. Daniel works closely with the managers. He identifies targets, works to get them and we are no different to other clubs in occasionally not being able to acquire who might be top of your list. Sometimes there's a degree of frustration [from Daniel] at how much is written that isn't accurate. But Daniel is so focused on delivering for this club. And that's why any of us who work around him think the criticism is grossly unfair."

Donna argued that "money doesn't guarantee you success" as she explained: "We've had seasons when we've brought eight players and it's not been right. What's key is we've still got so many young players. I remember years ago looking at our Under-16s, U17s and U18s and knowing a golden generation was coming through. They were the Harry Kanes and Harry Winks. We've still got young players. You saw Luke Amos play this week. The potential is still there, so why would you necessarily need to look so much further?"

Donna was speaking at an event in Los Angeles with First Star, a charity which helps foster youth. She said: "Children in care is one of the things we're really passionate about and 'To Care is To Do' is one of our long-running projects, one in which we invest a lot of time and energy." When asked if the £850m bill for the new stadium was impacting on transfers, Cullen said: "Not necessarily. The whole notion of us moving to an increased capacity is to collect the greater revenues from match day that other top-six clubs have been enjoying for many more years than ourselves."

Levy was passionate about the new stadium, and immensely proud when it finally opened after months of delay which played a heavily toll on his stress levels but a measure of that pride came through when Levy and a host of Tottenham academy players buried a time capsule filled with 'artefacts that capture the passions of White Hart Lane' at the club's new stadium. The capsule will be on view through a glass cover in the West Atrium section of the stadium and will form part of the stadium tour route that will become open to fans. Levy said: 'We are at a significant point in the club's history as we embark on our next chapter and prepare to enter a new home that will be enjoyed by future generations and our community for years to come. It is vitally important that we, as custodians of this great club, capture this moment in time and give future generations of players and supporters an insight into our thoughts and hopes during this exciting era. I am delighted that we were joined by members of our academy teams for this historic moment and hope that they are here in 50 years' time to open the capsule."

Publicly, at least, Pochettino backed his chairman when the stress was at its height. When there was anger from fans over delays to the near £1 billion project, Pochettino said: "The chairman is suffering a lot. He is so tired about work. The last few months he didn't sleep because he is trying to deliver the stadium. I think people don't realise the magnitude of the project and how difficult it is to manage. Everyone is disappointed because we are still not playing there but the day we move everyone is going to realise how massive the project was and how good the facilities are. It doesn't just depend on him. When you build something, you depend on many companies. I think it's more than 20 that are working there. It's so, so difficult. That is why he needs to feel the love from the fans and the club. He is working so hard, too hard, to leave a legacy for ever. And I think that's fantastic."

Pochettino, meanwhile, laughed off rumours of interest from Real Madrid. "I prefer that newspapers talk about things like this than, 'Tottenham is going to sack me', or 'people are tired of me'.

I don't get bored (with the speculation) but he (Levy) maybe is worried," joked Pochettino. "He suffers because he's jealous about me! It's normal, no? He's a very jealous person."

How times change? And oh so quickly. When Pochettino was coveted by Manchester United, and the media was full of stories about a potential move to Old Trafford, former manager Tim Sherwood made this observation on the Sky Sports Debate show, in mid-December 2018. "Daniel Levy will be worried because it's Manchester United, any other club in the Premier League, forget about it. I don't think he will go. I think he is halfway through building something very special. How will Daniel react to it? Daniel will dismiss it. You could give £200million at this present moment in time for Pochettino, Daniel Levy will turn that down."

Pochettino's relationship with his chairman was the subject of enormous debate with continuous conspiracy theories that all was not well behind the scenes when it came to the manager's vision of recruitment, once culminating in Pochettino stating that he was the "coach not the manager".

At another time Pochettino was far more reflective when he said, "I speak to him a lot, we talk a lot, we have very good communication. We don't always agree but, of course, that is normal. He is a person with a lot of experience managing this type of project and we are football people trying to advise on the decision on football. That means sometimes we agree and sometimes we don't agree. But after, when the decision is made, we are so strong in the delivery of it which shows it is best for the club. Many, many things happen in a football club, we are in contact nearly every day. On one side I listen more and agree with him, on another side he must agree with me in some decisions. But, always, we try to reach a compromise. He has one view, we have another. We are on different levels, of course he is my boss and then I need to respect him. At some point I need to convince him but when he wants to do something, because he's the boss, he doesn't need to convince me. Sometimes it looks like the board and the chairman are the worst enemy of the manager and the coaching staff, the football versus the financial side. But the relationship is good and

Spurs owner Joe Lewis (left) and chairman Daniel Levy

we always try to make the best decision for the club."

Levy had sacked managers before when they were under performing, and there might have been a small degree of sympathy for their exit by the fans. This time it was vastly different. He knew that the wailing and hysteria over the sacking of such a popular manager as Pochettino would vanish overnight with the appointment of someone so high profile and a serial trophy winner as Mourinho. Pochettino called for Levy to "be brave, take risks and work in a different way" after the final game of last season — widely interpreted as a plea for the chairman to release the financial shackles. Pochettino signed a five-year deal soon after, suggesting he had been placated with promises of money to spend.

Former Spurs centre forward Peter Crouch analysed both sacking and appointment when he said: "There was an issue. You look at the players at the start of the season, three or four big players wanting to leave. Why is that? Did they fall out with the manager? There were rumours about him watching training from upstairs and not coming out. I know some players in that dressing room were uncomfortable with what was going on.

"I have to say how cut-throat Daniel Levy can be; buying young players with resale value. As soon as you hit 30, and I know this from experience, I was out (signing for Stoke in 2011). There was no resale value. But Mourinho, the way he works, he likes 30-plus players. He doesn't mind age. If they're good enough, they're in. How are they (he and Levy) going to get on?"

However, while Levy is the man in the firing line, the actual owner of Spurs is Joe Lewis, effectively Levy's boss, and the man who makes all the major decisions. Lewis's best mate is Tiger Woods, who has called Joe "my business mentor" in the past. Each year, when he's not injured, Tiger takes part in Joe's Tavistock Cup competition in Florida, held on two of Joe's developments in Orlando called the Isleworth and Lake Nona. When Tiger Woods had his infamous 2009 low-speed car accident, it was at Joe's Isleworth complex, where the golfer has a home. Joe, who also owns property in Argentina and Bulgaria, lives next door to 007 legend Sean Connery, who he is reportedly close to. South African golfer Ernie Els is another pal, and the pair are said to regularly dine together. Joe plays off a 14 handicap and has practised with Woods and Els in the past.

The East End-born self-made billionaire had a new 321 foot-long, £112m masterpiece of a yacht delivered from famous shipyard Abeking and Rasmussen in Lemwerder in 2017, the vessel took nearly three years to build. The multi-million pound mega yacht Aviva – the owner's fourth yacht to bear the name – was built in strictly controlled conditions at the yard, with very little known about her interior design. While the majority of the super yacht's designs were shrouded in secrecy, *Boat International* suggests that Aviva has a full sized tennis court with rooms for up to 16 guests. Lewis's estimated net worth is around £4.09 billion according to *Forbes*, he is the fifth richest man in the UK, although the businessman, investor and art collector now resides in the Bahamas. He spends a great deal of his time travelling the world on business in his yachts, and reportedly has artwork by Paul Cezanne, Gustav Klimt and Picasso on board, worth £1bn plus. He paid £26.3 million for Francis Bacon's Triptych (1974-1977) painting.

Nicknamed "The Boxer" because of his sporting namesake, Lewis is a true cockney who was born within the sound of the St.

Joe Lewis's boat that is said to include a full-size indoor tennis court

Mary-le-Bow church bells in 1937, which makes him 82-years-old. Thought to have been raised in a flat above the Roman Arms pub in East London, Joe left school at 15-years-old to work in his family's cafe as a waiter earning £6 a week, later establishing businesses in London's West End under the name Tavistock Banqueting, he opened restaurants including the Northumberland Grand, which was the first fancy dress-themed eatery in London aimed at tourists.

He developed the Beefeater, the Cockney, the Caledonian and the Hanover Grand, and managed his first super club called The Talk of the Town in the 60s, where Frank Sinatra, Diana Ross and Tom Jones performed. At the Hanover Grand, Joe gave The Nolans their first ever live show and gave Planet Hollywood and Hard Rock founder Robert Earl his first job. He also moved into the world of tourist shops, selling souvenirs and laying on bus tours of London for tourists and dropping them off at his restaurants. He sold the business in 1979 for £30m and moved to the Bahamas as a tax exile. He set up home in Nassau, the capital of the islands and entered the world of currency trading, accumulating tens of millions, gambling on stock.

In September 1992 he became a billionaire, in part to one shrewd investment on Black Wednesday, teaming up with investor George Soros believing the Pound was overvalued and would collapse as Britain attempted to align it with other Euro countries.

He bet on the Pound crashing out of the European Exchange Rate Mechanism and as it did he became a billionaire overnight. He repeated the ploy many years later betting successfully against the Mexican peso.

Joe has been married twice, his first wife was Esther Browne who he met at his greasy spoon. She now lives in Ireland. They had two children, Vivienne and Charlie, before they divorced. Joe then married his former assistant Jane, they don't have any children.

In May 2013, Spurs went on a trip to the Bahamas and were welcomed on board the super yacht by host Joe. Michael Dawson, who was skipper at the time, said: "I had never met him before, so it was nice to go over there and a great experience. What a really nice guy. And that yacht is unreal! But he's just a normal guy. You could chat to him about anything. He tunes into all the games, he loves it. We just sat there chatting. He made us feel so welcome over there. It was relaxed. A lot of team-bonding together. It helps to be able to put a face to the person investing so much in this club he wants to be successful. He's always watching. He knows what goes on. He would remember every game, every little thing."

YEAR	NATIONALITY	MANAGER
1898	ENGLAND	FRANK BRETTELL
1899	SCOTLAND	JOHN CAMERON
1907	ENGLAND	FRED KIRKHAM
1912	SCOTLAND	PETER MCWILLIAM
1927	ENGLAND	BILLY MINTER
1930	ENGLAND	PERCY SMITH(C)
1935	ENGLAND	WALLY HARDINGE
1935	ENGLAND	JACK TRESADERN
1938	SCOTLAND	PETER MCWILLIAM
1942	ENGLAND	ARTHUR TURNER
1946	ENGLAND	JOE HULME
1949	ENGLAND	ARTHUR ROWE
1955	ENGLAND	JIMMY ANDERSON
1958	ENGLAND	BILL NICHOLSON
1974	NORTHERN IRELAND	TERRY NEILL
1976	ENGLAND	KEITH BURKINSHAW
1984	WALES	PETER SHREEVES
1986	ENGLAND	DAVID PLEAT
1987	ENGLAND	TREVOR HARTLEY (C)
1987	ENGLAND	DOUG LIVERMORE
1987	ENGLAND	TERRY VENABLES
1991	WALES	PETER SHREEVES
1992	ENGLAND	DOUG LIVERMORE & RAY CLEMENCE
1993	ARGENTINA	OSVALDO ARDILES
1994	ENGLAND	STEVE PERRYMAN (C)
1994	ENGLAND	GERRY FRANCIS
1997	REPUBLIC OF IRELAND	CHRIS HUGHTON (C)
1997	SWITZERLAND	CHRISTIAN GROSS
1998	ENGLAND	DAVID PLEAT (C)
1998	SCOTLAND	GEORGE GRAHAM
2001	ENGLAND	DAVID PLEAT (C)
2001	ENGLAND	GLENN HODDLE
2003	ENGLAND	DAVID PLEAT (C)
2004	FRANCE	JACQUES SANTINI
2004	NETHERLANDS	MARTIN JOL
2007	ENGLAND	CLIVE ALLEN & ALEX INGLETHORPE (C)
2007	SPAIN	JUANDE RAMOS
2008	ENGLAND	CLIVE ALLEN & ALEX INGLETHORPE (C)
2008	ENGLAND	HARRY REDKNAPP
2012	PORTUGAL	ANDRÉ VILLAS-BOAS
2013	ENGLAND	TIM SHERWOOD
2014	ARGENTINA	MAURICIO POCHETTINO
2019	PORTUGAL	JOSE MOURINHO

ABOUT THE AUTHOR

HARRY HARRIS HAS written numerous books on Spurs including Down Memory Lane and the life stories of Spurs managers Bill Nicholson, Glenn Hoddle, Terry Venables, Martin Jol and Terry Neill. He started out as a journalist at the *Tottenham Weekly Herald* in Tottenham High Road. He went onto become a double winner of the British Sports Journalist of the Year award with special affinity to the KIO cause, and winner of The Race In The Media award, the only football writer ever to do so.

Presented with the British Variety Club of Great Britain Silver Heart for 'Contribution to Sports Journalism'. he is also a double winner of the Sports Story of the Year award, the only journalist ever to win the Sports Story of the year accolade twice. Harry has a total of 24 industry awards.

A regular football analyst on TV news and sports programmes such as Richard & Judy, Newsnight, BBC News and ITV News at Ten he also appeared regularly on Sky Sports and Setanta Sports as well as Radio 5 Live, Radio 4, and TalkSport. Harry was interviewed on Football Focus, and was a founder member of the original Hold The Back Page and Jimmy Hill Sunday Supplement shows on Sky.

Arguably the most prolific writer of best-selling football books of his generation, among nearly 90 books are the highly acclaimed best sellers in the UK and the States *Pele - His Life and Times* and George Best's last book *Hard Tackles and Dirty Baths*. *Gullit: The Chelsea Diary*, *Chelsea Century*, *Chelski*, and *Wayne Rooney - The Story of Footballs Wonder Kid*. He has written the autobiography of Gary Mabbutt as well as books on Jurgen Klinsmann, Spurs Glory, Glory Nights in Europe, and four books on Jose Mourinho. Harry is one of the most influential football columnists for three decades, one of the most acclaimed investigative journalists and news gatherers of his generation and has worked for *Daily Mail, Daily Mirror, Daily Express, Daily Star, Sunday Express* and *Star on Sunday*, he has also been ESPNsoccernet Football Correspondent and contributed to BT Sport.

NEW BOOKS FOR 2020

THE KILLING OF EMILIANO SALA

KING KLOPP

FIRSTLY CONGRATULATIONS TO JOSÉ Mourinho for his appointment as Tottenham Hotspur Manager at a very exciting time in the club's history from all at Footba11legends Ltd. Footba11Legends Ltd trades in sports memorabilia, promotes Question & Answers evenings with football legends and is currently working on an online fanzine.

José Mourinho is a brilliant appointment from the Spurs board who want to convert the attractive football into winning a trophy in the near future. The last trophy Spurs won was The League Cup 2008 with Middlesbrough born Jonathan Woodgate scoring the winning goal. Coincidentally Tottenham have been drawn against Middlesbrough, now managed by Jonathan, in this season's FA Cup.

The FA Cup is a trophy which Spurs have a great history in with that magnificent goal scored by Ricky Villa in the 1981 final. Keith Burkinshaw managed an extremely talented side with every football fan wanting to score volleys like Glenn Hoddle and pass like Ossie Ardiles.

Now José has come in, he is a serial winner he and his teams can achieve anything. The way Dele Alli, Moussa Sissoko have been reinvigorated in the first few weeks of his reign is amazing. I think the English Premier League with José in it and the current great managers who are plying their trade make for an exciting second half to the 2019-2020 season. Good luck to Mauricio, I hope he is back in the Premier League in the near future, he is a talent. As Spurs and England Legend Jimmy Greaves would say "it's a funny

old game!" but it's also a results business.

Harry Harris is a true legend of sports journalism and a genuine objective Spurs fan. I have enjoyed reading some fabulous books written by Harry over the years. One that stands out is *Down Memory Lane* where the fans and players selected the Dream XI. My personal favourite legends are Glenn Hoddle, Steve Perryman, Ossie Ardiles, Ricky Villa, Paul Gascogne, Garry Lineker, Les Ferdinand and Pat Jennings.

José Mourinho has applied his undoubted positive attitude and belief to be a winner. He instils this self-belief in the teams he builds and knows only too well that tough and sometimes not popular decision need to be taken for the good of the team. He has already done this at Spurs, when Eric Dier was substituted on 29 minutes against Olympiakos with Spurs 2-0 down. José reiterating it wasn't a reflection on Eric's performance but it was what the team needed at that moment. The final result, a 4-2 win to secure last 16 of The Champions League, underlined the correctness in his thinking. You cannot win Trophies, League titles and Champions League trophies without strong characters and leaders on the field of play.

In Harry Kane José has a leader. It's unusual for a forward to be captain and Harry does this for Club and Country. I have been fortunate to spend time in the company of Spurs and England, TV Pundit and living legend Glenn Hoddle. I asked Glenn about the captain's role he reminded me that a captain needs to have the respect of the team and be able to galvanise the group on the pitch which is what Harry Kane does every game similar to Glenn's England Captain Alan Shearer.

Alan Shearer is currently The Premier League's all time top scorer with 260 goals, a record which Harry Kane could eventually overhaul. They are two great players who stayed loyal to their clubs. I hope Harry can add some silverware to go with his loyalty.

Good Luck to José Mourinho - The Boss!

Ant Verrill

@footba11legends

Printed in Poland
by Amazon Fulfillment
Poland Sp. z o.o., Wrocław

54339421R00116